SCOTN(
Numbe

The Poetry of
Sorley MacLean

Emma Dymock

Association for Scottish Literary Studies 2011

Published by
Association for Scottish Literary Studies
Scottish Literature
7 University Gardens
University of Glasgow
Glasgow G12 8QH
www.asls.org.uk

ASLS is a registered charity no. SC006535

First published 2011

A CIP catalogue for this title
is available from the British Library

ISBN 978-1-906841-05-8

The Association for Scottish Literary Studies
acknowledges the support of Creative Scotland
towards the publication of this book.

CONTENTS

SCOTNOTES

Study guides to major Scottish writers and literary texts

Produced by the Education Committee
of the Association for Scottish Literary Studies

Series Editors
Lorna Borrowman Smith
Ronald Renton

Editorial Board
Ronald Renton, St Aloysius' College, Glasgow
(Convener, Education Committee, ASLS)
Jim Alison, HMI (retired)
Professor John Corbett, University of Glasgow
Dr Emma Dymock, University of Edinburgh
Dr Morna Fleming, Liberton High School
Professor Douglas Gifford, University of Glasgow
John Hodgart, Garnock Academy
Alan MacGillivray, Past President of ASLS
Catrina McGillivray, Newbattle Abbey College
Dr David Manderson, University of the West of Scotland
Dr Christopher Nicol, Galashiels Academy
Lorna Ramsay, Fairlie, Ayrshire
Professor Alan Riach, University of Glasgow
Dr Christine Robinson, Scottish Language Dictionaries
Dr Kenneth Simpson, University of Strathclyde
Lorna Borrowman Smith, formerly Wallace High School

THE ASSOCIATION FOR SCOTTISH LITERARY STUDIES
aims to promote the study, teaching and writing of Scottish
literature, and to further the study of the languages of
Scotland.

To these ends, the ASLS publishes works of Scottish
literature; literary criticism and in-depth reviews of Scottish
books in *Scottish Literary Review*; short articles, features
and news in *ScotLit*; and scholarly studies of language in
Scottish Language. It also publishes *New Writing Scotland*,
an annual anthology of new poetry, drama and short fiction,
in Scots, English and Gaelic. ASLS has also prepared a
range of teaching materials covering Scottish language and
literature for use in schools.

All the above publications are available as a single 'package',
in return for an annual subscription. Enquiries should be
sent to:

ASLS
Scottish Literature
7 University Gardens
University of Glasgow
Glasgow G12 8QH

Tel/fax +44 (0)141 330 5309
e-mail **office@asls.org.uk**
or visit our website at **www.asls.org.uk**

INTRODUCTION

In *O Choille gu Bearradh: Collected Poems*, Sorley MacLean asserts that 'In spite of MacDiarmid, the 'full-time' professional poet is not for me and never has been. If I have time to do it, I brood over something until a rhythm comes, as a more or less tight rope to cross the abyss of silence.' Like many of MacLean's statements about himself, this could be viewed as both illuminating and misleading. For while MacLean's poetic output throughout his life was not always relentless – as a teacher, his ability to 'harness the Muse' must often have been challenged due to the pressures and demands of work – his belief in his role as a poet, and in particular, his role as a Gaelic poet, never wavered.

Sorley MacLean is one of the most important poets of the 20th century in Scotland. He was a Gaelic speaker and, as a speaker of this minority language, he also campaigned for Gaelic to be better recognised in schools and beyond. In 1911, the year of MacLean's birth, there were 202,398 Gaelic speakers but by 1931, when MacLean was attending university and beginning to realise his talent as a poet, the numbers had decreased to 136,135. The sharp decrease was largely due to the losses of Gaelic-speaking young men after World War I. The numbers of speakers continued to fall considerably during the rest of the 20th century, but nevertheless, Gaelic remains an important part of Scotland's culture and its literature is an important aspect of its continued appeal for Gaelic speakers and non-Gaelic speakers alike. The Scottish Gaelic poetic tradition is long established and its history stretches back to a time when Scottish Gaelic and Irish were one language and when bards were held in high esteem as professional tradition-bearers. The bardic poetry, which was formal and strict in form and metre, was part of a learned tradition which included elegies, panegyric poetry (the praising of the chief) and satire, but there also flourished a song tradition which was more diverse in scope and content. Much of the poetry survived due to oral transmission and was later written down. By the 18th and 19th centuries, Gaelic poetry was also being used to transmit political senti-

1

ment regarding the Jacobite Rising, the Clearances, and the Land Agitation.

MacLean's influence on the scope and direction of Gaelic poetry is immeasurable but he did not exist within a vacuum and he was certainly not exclusively influenced by his Gaelic tradition. His poetry must also be studied within the context of the Scottish Renaissance and the influence that European politics had on the poets of the 1930s and 1940s. MacLean can be viewed as an international poet because, like the poetry of Hugh MacDiarmid, his work transcends issues of local identity and nationality and deals with eternal themes. Yet his imagery and symbolism never veer too far from his own landscape, thus ensuring that his own experience informs the various philosophical ideas he strives to understand and align himself with. He is known to be a love poet, a political poet, a poet whose work is based on polarity and a poet whose work spans both tradition and innovation. While these descriptions are all correct, this little book will attempt to study the actual poems which are responsible for them and to make sense of the various strands which span MacLean's poems throughout his life, offering some insight into the context of his work and providing close readings of some of the poetry which is most representative of his themes and ideas.

The very nature of MacLean's poetry means that it is often difficult to capture in the space of one book the myriad ideas which are latent in his work. His most obvious themes will therefore be dealt with in detail and other secondary ideas and theories will be mentioned in conjunction with these. Where appropriate, the multi-faceted aspect of MacLean's symbols will be explored so that the reader may understand the many possibilities underlying the poetry. This book could be used as both a general introduction and a starting point from which to study the poetry more deeply. MacLean composed his poems in Gaelic but he also provided translations which are often very literal. This book is for the benefit of those who are interested in the poetry of MacLean whether they understand Gaelic or not, but obviously, translation can be a thorny issue, especially when meaning can be watered down or lost between languages. For this reason, in many of the discussions in this book I have concentrated on the meaning of the poetry in a historical, socio-political and literary context, instead of a specific and detailed exploration of Gaelic language. Some of the critical essays by other scholars, which I have listed in the bibliography, deal more specifically with Gaelic language for those interested in deepening their understanding of this area of study.

Biographical Details

Sorley MacLean was born on Raasay in 1911 and was raised in Osgaig, Raasay. He was one of a family of seven. From an early age he was influenced by Gaelic tradition on both sides of his family – he particularly remembers his father's mother singing the great Gaelic songs to him and his aunt on his mother's side of the family knew many of the songs of Mairi Mhòr (Mary MacPherson, a famous 19th century Gaelic poet from Skye). According to MacLean he was not a singer himself but he compensated for this with a sensitive understanding of rhythm and time – he even suggests that his decision to become a poet was based on the fact that he could not sing. It is worth noting that MacLean's love of the 'old songs' and the fact that his family had such a rich background in Gaelic oral culture was often at odds with Raasay's strong Free Presbyterian tradition. MacLean shows that the two do not always sit well together when he emphasises the fact that his mother's family had 'learned many old songs from their MacLeod mother ... even though she was a pious "adherent" of the Free Presbyterian Church.' This tension between the Gaelic oral tradition and the Free Presbyterian Church may have been one of the reasons why MacLean grew critical of the church from a relatively young age. He writes that his scepticism about the Church's politics 'seeped through the protective walls of the individual very early and made for pessimism and I believe toleration and a sympathy for the underdog ... At the age of 12 I took to the gospel of socialism ...'

MacLean chose to study Honours English Language and Literature as opposed to Honours Celtic at Edinburgh University because it was 'economically disastrous' to take

Celtic. Most of the positions in Celtic departments at that time were filled by young academics[1] and thus jobs would be scarce once MacLean had graduated. MacLean gained a First Class degree in English and it was during these years that he was able to explore English literature properly for the first time. He familiarised himself with the work of such writers as W.B.Yeats, T.S.Eliot, Ezra Pound and Hugh MacDiarmid as well as movements in literature such as Romanticism and Modernism. He continued his studies at Moray House, the Edinburgh teacher training college, and around this time was introduced to C.M. Grieve (Hugh MacDiarmid) in Rutherford's Bar. A friendship soon flourished between the two men. MacDiarmid was greatly impressed with the work of contemporary Gaelic poets and championed their work – he was already looking to Gaelic Scotland for the voice of an authentic Scottish identity, so the emergence of the talents of MacLean as well as George Campbell Hay came at the right time for him.

In 1934 MacLean took up his first teaching post in Portree Secondary School, helping to finance the education of his younger brothers and sisters. This was during the time of the Depression and his choice to go into teaching may have been influenced by the economic recession. By 1938 MacLean was teaching English at Tobermory Secondary School on Mull and it was here that he was able to view the full extent of the Clearances and how this period in Highland history had affected the people and the culture – this realisation can only have helped to fuel his socialist ideals. The Spanish Civil War had already begun in 1936 and MacLean's urge was to fight against fascism on the Republican side. In his love poetry *Dàin do Eimhir/ Poems to Eimhir* he gives the impression that he would choose the love of 'Eimhir' over his duty to fight but in reality it was more for economic reasons that he remained in Scotland as a teacher.

'An Cuilithionn' was begun by MacLean in the spring of 1939 and was his attempt at a long poem in the same vein as MacDiarmid's *A Drunk Man Looks at the Thistle*. During this time he was keeping a close eye on political events and he took up a teaching post at Boroughmuir High School. MacLean was able to renew contacts within literary circles during this time and often attended meetings with Robert Garioch in the Abbotsford Bar in Rose Street. Many poets and intellectuals met there, including Sydney Goodsir Smith and Alexander Scott. It was at this time MacLean and Garioch collaborated on the poetry collection, *Seventeen Poems for Sixpence*. Also during this period MacLean got to know Douglas Young who was a gifted classical scholar, a poet and a man of strong political commitment. For nationalist reasons Young did not fight in WWII but, nevertheless, MacLean and Young found much common ground in relation to literature and their hopes for the future of Gaelic.

When World War II broke out MacLean could not enlist as a volunteer immediately for family reasons and between October 1939 and June 1940 he taught evacuees in Hawick. On 26th September 1940 MacLean left Edinburgh for military training at Catterick Camp in Yorkshire and in December 1941 he was sent to Egypt on active service as a member of the Signal Corps. His experiences of war fuelled many of his poems that were written around this time, and while he was overseas Young looked after the manuscripts of *Dàin do Eimhir* and 'An Cuilithionn', preparing them for publication and consulting MacLean in his letters about grammar and other queries regarding the poems. After MacLean was wounded at the Battle of El Alamein in November 1942 he had to recover in military hospital and was eventually discharged from Raigmore Hospital, Inverness in August 1943. He continued teaching at Boroughmuir High School after the war and in 1946 he married Renee Cameron. They began their life together in Edinburgh and in 1947 he was promoted to Principal Teacher of English at Boroughmuir High School. In February 1956 he moved to Plockton in Wester Ross where he was Headmaster of Plockton High School from 1956 to his retirement in 1972.

MacLean did not publish his verse continuously throughout his life. Although this may be partly due to the pressures of teaching, it may also be connected to his personal view of poetry. According to MacLean himself, he did not believe in art for art's sake and he composed poetry only when

something moved him to the extent that he felt compelled
to write. As well as the publication of *Dàin do Eimhir agus
Dain Eile* in 1943, *Reothairt is Contraigh / Spring tide and
Neap tide: Selected poems 1932–72* was published in 1977
and *O Choille gu Bearradh / From Wood to Ridge: Collected
Poems* in 1989. He retired to the Braes district of Skye,
was Writer in Residence at Edinburgh University for two
years and received Honorary Degrees from seven universi-
ties. Sorley MacLean died in 1996. His poetic achievement
ensures that 20th century Gaelic verse can never be viewed
as inward looking or even exclusively 'Scotland-centred'. His
symbols provide meanings that are as significant to the rest
of Europe as they are to the Highlands and Islands.

Political and Literary Influences
on Sorley MacLean's Poetry
Socialism and Communism: One of the main intellectual
forces which writers and poets were influenced by during
the 1920s and 1930s was socialism. Many of the Scottish
intelligentsia were left-wing in their political vision and
students during the 1930s were looking towards Europe for
inspiration and were taking an internationalist stance – the
writings of Marx and Engels were being read. Many Scottish
students caught up in the passionate idealism of the late
1930s joined the communists going out to fight on the side
of the Republicans during the Spanish Civil War and buses
picked up people in Edinburgh and Glasgow for this specific
purpose. MacLean himself expressed a desire to fight in the
Spanish Civil War. However, this idealism fuelled by poets
and writers also stemmed from real issues in Scotland at
this time. After the First World War the social and economic
consequences of Scotland's narrow industrial base could be
easily seen. The Clyde shipbuilding industry suffered greatly
during the Great Depression and Lloyd George's promise
that the soldiers of the Great War would return to a land
fit for heroes had come to nothing. One of Sorley MacLean's
heroes, John MacLean, is synonymous with 'Red Clydeside',
and, while he was an inspirational figure to the workers, for
the Government at Westminster he symbolised the danger

of Bolshevism that was thought to be threatening Britain. Sorley MacLean joined the British Army and fought during WWII, but he never lost his communist ideals and he followed the progress of the Soviet Union with great interest. He became disillusioned when the atrocities of Stalin became public knowledge but, in spite of this, even his later poems show signs of socialist idealism.

Scottish Nationalism, Hugh MacDiarmid and the Scottish Renaissance: Hugh MacDiarmid was a central figure of the Scottish literary scene during the 1930s and younger poets like MacLean were fully aware of his importance even though MacDiarmid had not been so readily accepted by the Establishment. MacDiarmid's early career as a poet and writer is associated with issues of national identity and Scottish literature, dating to well before the time that MacLean and his friends knew him. Celtic Romantics and cultural nationalists took their lead from the growth of Irish nationalism in the 1920s, which was also a movement with very close links to its national literature and culture. Scottish cultural nationalists were often at odds with more politically minded nationalists, who were more intent on pursuing Home Rule and were concerned that 'Romantic' nationalists would take away the focus from their goal. Nevertheless, cultural rebirth was happening at the same time as these political changes in Scotland. MacDiarmid was to play a major role in this revival to such an extent that his name has become synonymous with the Scottish Literary Renaissance. He viewed the cultural revival as being intrinsic to the struggle for a separate political identity. He concentrated on bringing to the fore a distinctively Scottish poetry written in Scots and he also looked towards Gaelic Scotland for inspiration. The effect his poetry had on Scottish identity was of major significance. Sorley MacLean has made it clear that MacDiarmid's poetry, with its modern aesthetic, greatly affected his own view of poetry and MacLean's attempt at a long poem, 'An Cuilithionn', was partly inspired by MacDiarmid's *A Drunk Man Looks at the Thistle* (1926) in which he attacks the Scottish Establishment and then attempts to define the Scottish character.

Modernist Concepts of Self: As a 20ᵗʰ century movement, Modernism affected visual art, music and literature and it clearly influenced MacLean's poetry in a variety of ways. MacLean's poetry can be viewed as groundbreaking, achieving effects that had never been fully realised in Gaelic poetry before that time. One of the most 'modern' aspects of his work is the way in which he explores the concept of self. When MacLean was a student, he and his friends George Davie and James Caird would have explored during discussions the notion of the self within philosophical systems, with its divisions of the mind and spirit. The influences of Freudian and Jungian psychoanalysis, alongside the philosophical theories of Descartes, Hume, Locke, and Kant may have had an impact on young intellectuals and may have affected the way in which identity was portrayed in literature. Certainly, writers such as T.S. Eliot and the French Symbolists were opening up the possibilities of how identity could be represented and deciphered. The idea of the self – mind, body and spirit – was a significant idea and one that was unavoidable for any literary minded intellectual in the 20ᵗʰ century. This subject had been a matter of debate since the Romantic poets had presented the idea of the 'divided self' – poets were faced with the paradox of the man of action and inaction, especially after the Romantics had developed the concept of introspection and placed a greater emphasis on subjectivity. These ideas filtered into the poetry that MacLean began to compose. However, while the concept of the self was important to MacLean, because of his socialist stance he was also exploring his place within the collective. This exploration was not just influenced by socialism but also stemmed from his identity as a Gael. The 'collectivity' of the clan system, while not nearly as powerful as it had been centuries before, was still strongly felt by many Gaels and MacLean was well aware that he came from a rich tradition in which song and poetry played an important part in the history and the present lives of his people. Many of his poems involve MacLean looking back at past centuries and the poetry of his predecessors. This was not solely a Gaelic concern – T.S. Eliot's influential essay 'Tradition and the

Individual Talent' (1919) also explores the tension between the sense of individuality and the influence and knowledge of a wider literary heritage.

Recurring Themes in MacLean's Poetry

Throughout this book I will be referring to recurring themes in MacLean's work. Often specific themes and symbols overlap and for this reason it is impossible to separate MacLean's poetry into sections such as 'love poetry' and 'political poetry'. The themes covered in many of the main discussions will include MacLean's view of the role of the poet; concepts of Gaelic identity; polarity and tension in his work, including the choice between political duty and love; landscape symbolism; the concept of heroic self sacrifice; the quest for self identity and the striving for transcendence. Rather than discuss MacLean's themes in a general manner, I have chosen to concentrate mainly on close readings of a selection of MacLean's poetry to show the way in which his themes are explored throughout his work.

Poetic Style and Metre

John MacInnes has written that 'A large part of Somhairle MacGill-Eain's greatness as a poet lies in his restorative work: this can properly be celebrated as a triumph of regeneration ... his poetry is intensely Gaelic even when it is so different from anything else in Gaelic'. It should be noted that MacLean's poetry shows signs of being greatly influenced by the Gaelic poetry of previous centuries, from both the bardic tradition and the song tradition which MacLean fondly refers to as the 'old songs'. Thus most of MacLean's metrical patterns are Gaelic or, at the very least, a mix of Gaelic and English forms. While his stanza forms and rhyme patterns often remain regular, the imagery and symbolism which he employs within the poetry result in it appearing completely original. One of the most obvious techniques which MacLean uses to very good effect is the changing of speed and rhythm and the shape of stanzas in different sections of the same poem. This affects the pace of the poem but can also give the reader a significant understanding of the different voices in a long poem such as 'An Cuilithionn'. In particular, this is evident in Part VI of the poem in which the voice of the Gesto girl uses a different metre from the voice of Clio, the Muse of history. Although the metres may be traditional there is something inherently modern about using them in this way, especially when we take into consideration how modernist writers employ a multitude of fragmented voices and speech patterns. This results in a sense of timelessness rather than a continuous singular voice set firmly in the present. Often MacLean matches the metre to his subject: the traditional praise of the landscape in 'An Cuilithionn', for example, is given in simple strophic form, a metre which is usually associated with 17th century Gaelic poets such as Iain Lom or Mary MacLeod. Sorley MacLean was also interested in what he called the 'lyric peaks' of poetry, which he found in MacDiarmid's *A Drunk Man Looks at the Thistle*: 'It converted me to the belief that the long medley with lyric peaks was the form for our age.'[2] Interestingly, MacLean's friend George Davie has suggested that MacLean's own 'lyric peaks', such as the Stallion section in 'An Cuilithionn Part V, are the high points in which his poetry is at its most 'Gaelic'. MacLean perhaps attests to this in his essay 'My Relationship with the Muse' when he writes that 'I could not be primarily a Gael without a very deep-seated conviction that the auditory is the primary sensuousness of poetry.' It is this sensuousness of poetry that MacLean is constantly striving for and therefore it makes sense for him to 'shun free verse' in favour of more 'Gaelic' forms of metre from his native tradition.

A Note on the Text and Layout
All poetry that is referred to throughout this book is taken from Sorley MacLean's *O Choille gu Bearradh / From Wood to Ridge: Collected Poems* unless otherwise stated. The translations are also taken from *O Choille gu Bearradh* and are MacLean's own. Page numbers refer to the corrected 1999 edition of the book, published by Carcanet/Birlinn. I have dedicated the whole of Chapter 1 to a discussion of *Dàin do Eimhir / Poems to Eimhir*, and the poems which are dealt with in detail in Chapter 2 are from the *Dàin Eile / Other Poems*

section in *Dàin do Eimhir*. In Chapter 3 MacLean's longest poem, 'An Cuilithionn', will be discussed, in Chapter 4 his war poetry will be assessed, and the remaining chapters will be dedicated to his later poems. I have picked out some of the main pivotal points of MacLean's work and have aimed to achieve a balance between his groundbreaking and influential early poetry and his important later work. Many other poems have not been given major attention because of the limits of space. Where relevant, I have mentioned some of these poems in the 'Further Reading' section at the end of each chapter in order to give readers both a sense of the breadth of MacLean's poetry and the way in which certain poems link into others. The main poems which are referred to throughout this Scotnote are dealt with in chronological order where possible. However, it is important to remember that, while MacLean's work can be studied chronologically, in many cases his themes and symbols can be traced throughout much of his poetry irrespective of timeframe.

Notes

1 Joy Hendry, 'Sorley MacLean: The Man and his Work' in *Sorley MacLean: Critical Essays*, ed. by Raymond J. Ross and Joy Hendry (Edinburgh: Scottish Academic Press, 1986) pp. 9–38 (p. 12).

2 MacLean, Sorley, 'My Relationship with the Muse' in *Ris a' Bhruthaich: The Criticism and Prose Writings of Sorley MacLean*, ed. by William Gillies (Stornoway: Acair, 1985) 6–14 (p. 11).

1. DÀIN DO EIMHIR/ POEMS TO EIMHIR – PURSUING THE MUSE ACROSS THE LANDSCAPE OF LOVE

Before analysing the content of *Dàin do Eimhir/ Poems to Eimhir*, it is necessary to look briefly at the effect that this collection had on the Gaelic world in general. It is not an understatement that *Dàin do Eimhir* changed Gaelic poetry completely – today the poems are still utterly modern but in 1943, when *Dàin do Eimhir* was first published, it caused something of a revolution in the way that Gaels viewed their own poetry and how it was perceived by the outside world. John MacInnes has written that people remember where they were when they first came into contact with the book and it is also fair to say that a good number of Gaelic learners were first moved to learn Gaelic in order to better understand these poems in their original language, such was the effect of these poems on the non-Gaelic speaking Scottish literati. To add to *Dàin do Eimhir's* reputation as a significant marker-stone of Modernism in Gaelic, the collection was first published with surrealist illustrations to accompany some of the poems by the artist William Crosbie. For the majority of the early readers of *Dàin do Eimhir*, these illustrations reinforced the idea that this collection was both a departure from what had gone before, and a new, groundbreaking creation in Gaelic poetry. The illustrations were certainly controversial for readers who had previously viewed Gaelic poetry as being strongly connected with Romanticism and the poems coupled with the illustrations took many Gaels outside their 'comfort zone'. However, when *Dàin do Eimhir* is surveyed as a whole, it is clear that Sorley MacLean was not simply attempting to ruffle feathers for the sake of controversy or even seeking notoriety by creating a modernist masterpiece for Gaelic. In reality, *Dàin do Eimhir* is the product of a mind which was equally sympathetic to a traditional Gaelic mindset and a modern European one – it came naturally to MacLean to combine these two elements to achieve something entirely new. This polarity, which at times achieves transcendence, is one of the defining factors of *Dàin do Eimhir*.

Dàin do Eimhir consists of sixty poems addressed to 'Eimhir' who, in Irish myth, was the wife of the great heroic figure Cù Chulainn. However, while use of 'Eimhir' as an image manages to connect to a real and imagined Gaelic tradition, shared by Ireland and Scotland, Eimhir also acts as a symbol of the Muse for MacLean in these poems and also operates as a smokescreen for the real women who inspired them. While these poems should be assessed as literature rather than biographical milestones, it is nevertheless useful to have some idea of their genesis. It is generally accepted that *Dàin do Eimhir* is mainly addressed to at least two different women – a fair-haired Irish girl and a red-haired Scottish girl. This in itself highlights the connection between Ireland and Scotland of which the poet is so aware, but in reality these were real women to whom MacLean was drawn in the 1930s. (There are actually thought to have been four 'Eimhirs' – the first two women are referred to in *Dàin* I, II and III). He fell in love with Nessa Ní Sheaghdha, an Irish woman, at a Celtic Congress in Edinburgh in 1937. She was conducting research in the National Library of Scotland. MacLean kept his feelings for her private, mistakenly thinking another of his friends wished to marry her. She married someone else in December 1939. A considerable number of the poems in *Dàin do Eimhir* are inspired by his feelings for this woman and, while his love for her was unrequited, she became a muse-like figure for the poet and her presence in his poetry allowed him to explore ideas and feelings that would otherwise have been difficult for him to harness without the strong emotions she inspired. In many ways this 'Eimhir' had a positive effect on his poetry, even if nothing came of his love for her in real life. One of the most famous of MacLean's 'Eimhir' poems inspired by the Irish woman is *Dàin* XIII, 'A Bhuaile Ghrèine/ The Sunny Fold', in which MacLean conjures up many famous lovers from myth, history and literature:

Do m' shùilean-sa bu tu Deirdre
's i bòidheach 's a' bhuaile ghrèine;
bu tu bean Mhic Ghille Bhrìghde
ann an àilleachd a lìthe.

Bu tu nighean bhuidhe Chòrnaig
is Mairearad an Amadain Bhòidhich,
an Una aig Tòmas Làidir,
Eimhir Chù-chulainn agus Gràinne,

To my eyes you were Deirdre
beautiful in the sunny cattle-fold;
you were MacBride's wife
in her shining beauty.
You were the yellow-haired girl of Cornaig
and the Handsome Fool's Margaret,
Strong Thomas's Una,
Cuchulainn's Eimhir and Grainne.
(pp. 12–13)

Deirdre is the 'Helen of Troy' in Irish myth while MacBride's
wife refers to Maud Gonne, whom the poet W.B. Yeats greatly
loved and admired. The girl of Cornaig is a familiar figure
in Gaelic song. She was killed by her brothers when she
wanted to marry a man they did not like. Margaret, another
figure from Gaelic song, was loved by the 'handsome fool',
but his mother tricked him into shooting Margaret, who
was washing by the river, by telling him that the girl was a
swan. 'Strong Thomas', or Thomas Costello as he is otherwise known, was prevented from marrying his love, Una
MacDermott, by Una's father. She later died. Gràinne was
another woman from Irish mythology whose story is similar
to Deirdre's. The list continues as the poem progresses –
MacLean is effectively mythologising his 'Eimhir' and he is
also placing himself within the canon of tormented lovers,
despite stating near the end of the poem that he is not one of
them. This poem is also a paean to music and poetry and one
wonders if MacLean views the coupling of love and sorrow
as the perfect condition for poetry, creating a drive and a
powerful energy:

's e mo chàs-sa an iargain
a ghabhas spiorad nam bàrd cianail
a ghlacadh anns na ranna pianta,

a thogail 's a chumail mar a b' àill leam
dìreach, cuimir anns an dàn dhut,

it is my dilemma to seize
in tormented verses the longing
that takes the spirit of sad poets,
to raise and keep as I would like,
direct and well-formed in the poem for you,
(pp. 14–15)

While MacLean is clear that he does not include himself
with the men he has listed in the poem, he views his role as
poet as important in capturing the beauty and longing of love
in order to preserve it in honour of his Muse and in honour of
the very essence of love. The sense of the unattainable is, in
the case of the figure of the Irish woman, a force for good in
MacLean's poetry, at least in respect of the calibre of poetry
he was producing.

The story attached to the red-haired Scottish woman is altogether a more thorny issue and this is reflected in the poems
that can be attributed to this specific period. Within the oral
tradition surrounding this poetry, it is assumed that the
Scottish woman is someone MacLean knew in his teens and
that in the August or September of 1939 he became strongly
attracted to her and declared his love for her. She appears
to have informed him that she could not have a full relationship with a man because of an operation and the scholar
Christopher Whyte has pointed out that the lines in *Dàin do
Eimhir* XLVII indicate the likelihood that the operation the
Scottish woman described to MacLean was an illegal abortion:

Carson, a Dhia, nach d' fhuair mi 'n cothrom,
mun d' shrac an t-òigear Goill do bhlàth,
mun d' rinneadh culaidh-thruais dhe d' bhòidhche

Why, God, did I not get the chance
before the young Lowlander tore your bloom,
before your beauty was made a thing of pity.
(pp. 148–149)

The imagery of mutilation and ebb and flood tides is also present in *Dàin do Eimhir* XL. MacLean uses the neap tide as a symbol of Eimhir's predicament:

Marbh-shruth na conntraigh 'nad chom ciùrrte
nach lìon ri gealaich ùir no làin,
anns nach tig reothairt mhòr an t-sùgraidh –
ach sìoladh dùbailt gu muir-tràigh.

Dead stream of neap in your tortured body,
which will not flow at new moon or at full,
in which the great springtide of love will not come –
But a double subsidence to lowest ebb.
(pp. 140–141)

The inference here is that the natural course cannot be taken – after every ebb tide there is the promise of a flood tide but in Eimhir's case there is no hope of this. The tides are clearly symbols of passion and, bearing in mind what MacLean had heard from the Scottish woman, it is likely that this poem is hinting at the impossibility of physical passion, especially with the mention of the woman's tortured body. Douglas Sealy has drawn attention to MacLean's reworking of the old song 'Mo Run Geal Dileas' about John MacLean holding off his passion for the Campbell woman. The words of the old traditional song cited below are much more optimistic than MacLean's own first stanza of his poem.

Cha bhi mi 'strìth ris a' chraoibh nach lùb leam
ged chinneadh ùbhlan air bhàrr gach gèig;
mo shoraidh slàn leat ma rinn thu m' fhàgail,
cha d' thàinig tràigh gun mhuir-làn 'n a dèigh.

I am not striving with the tree that will not bend for me,
although apples should grow on top of each branch;
farewell to me if you have left me,
no ebb came without a floodtide after it.[1]

In MacLean's poem apples do not grow on every branch and no flood follows the ebb tide. His line 'cha shoraidh slàn leat, cha d' rinn thu m' fhàgail:/ I do not bid you farewell, you did not leave me:' (pp. 140–141) is particularly descriptive of the poet's situation in 1941, in which he loves 'Eimhir' but has knowledge of her situation and the impossibility of consummating a relationship. It is evident that by using traditional Gaelic songs and reworking them in his own verse MacLean is not only paying tribute to his tradition but also viewing his predicament with Eimhir as being part of a tapestry which incorporates and echoes many of the tragic Gaelic figures of his tradition. In *Dàin do Eimhir* XLVI, which also emphasises the imagery of a wounded body, MacLean's own 'narrative' is emphasised and it is in a poem like this that the reader can really glimpse MacLean's very conscious awareness of the poetic sequence and his personal story within the poetry:

> Tha sinn còmhla, a ghaoil,
> leinn fhìn ann an Dùn-èideann,
> [...]
> ach le do thruaighe-sa tha m' ghaol
> air dhol 'na chaoir ghil leumraich,
> a' losgadh am bruaillean mo chinn
> mo chuimhne air an tèile,
> air tè nas rathaile 's nas bòidhche
> 's i pòsda thall an Eirinn.

> *We are together, dear,*
> *alone in Edinburgh,*
> *[...]*
> *but with your misery my love*
> *turns to white leaping flame,*
> *burning in the turmoil of my head*
> *my memory of the other,*
> *of a more fortunate and more lovely one*
> *who is married over in Ireland.*
> (pp. 146–149)

This poem was originally withheld from publication and was not published until 1970, presumably because it revealed too much personal detail for MacLean at the time. It also succeeds in exposing the fact that there is more than one Eimhir and that they existed at the same time in MacLean's own mind, almost vying for his attention. This poem is full of contrasts between the situation of one woman and the other but beyond the specifics there is another aspect to it – it may not be a direct reworking of an old song as in *Dàin do Eimhir* XL, but, while obviously being very firmly set in the poet's present life, it has the tone, honest style and subject matter of one of the Gaelic 'old songs' with its emphasis on basic information which has beneath its surface a richness of emotion and drama, bordering on the tragic. If this is indeed the case, MacLean is not only deliberately aligning himself with the traditional practice of narrating events but is also conscious of acting out events that he perhaps viewed as having a Gaelic or even universal aspect attached to them.

This narration of events being incorporated into wider, more universal issues is also true in relation to the earliest poems in *Dàin do Eimhir* which deal with MacLean's self-imposed sense of duty to fight in the Spanish Civil War against fascism. In 'Gaoir na h-Eòrpa/ The Cry of Europe' (IV) MacLean struggles with the choice he has to make, setting up his sense of duty in opposition to his love for Eimhir. In other poems of this same period such as 'An Roghainn/ The Choice' (XXII) he then berates himself for his lack of action, viewing himself as being unworthy of Eimhir because he did not go to Spain:

Cha d' ghabh mise bàs croinn-ceusaidh
an èiginn chruaidh na Spàinn
is ciamar sin bhiodh dùil agam
ri aon duais ùir an dàin?

I did not take a cross's death
in the hard extremity of Spain
and how then should I expect
the one new prize of fate?
(pp. 22–23)

In this same poem MacLean imagines himself to be walking out by the sea when, in surreal fashion, his reason asks him if it is true that his love is getting married on Monday, thereby suggesting that he has lost Eimhir and that this is somehow tied into his choice not to enlist. He believes he would have lost her either way because if he had died in Spain he would not have been able to experience her love, but the fact he now deems himself unworthy means she is lost to him anyway. In actuality it was for family reasons that MacLean did not fight in Spain. However, this does not mean that the conflict which plays out in his poetry is irrelevant – not only does it add a sense of drama to his love poetry but it also succeeds in giving him a better understanding of his own self. He writes in the introduction to *O Choille gu Bearradh* that 'Family reasons kept me from Spain in 1936–37, but in my heart of hearts I knew then that I "preferred a woman to crescent history", and was frank about it.' The philosophical debates that influence his poetry are no less significant even if they do not always fully match up with true biographical details and events. It is in these poems that we can glimpse MacLean exercising his poetic voice and exploring his concept of self and his role as a poet. Christopher Whyte describes it thus: 'The *Dàin do Eimhir* are not just a narrative of frustrated love, but also a conscious record of the realisation of a literary vocation.'

While the events attached to his dealings with the different Eimhir figures clearly had a major personal effect on the poet, the fact that these events produced poetry which often soared far beyond them should also not be forgotten. *Dàin do Eimhir* has the capacity to be both a cathartic journey into past and present events and also an exploration of greater collective truths, using human experience as a starting point. MacLean later found out in July 1941 that the Scottish woman's story had been untrue and he was understandably distressed about this situation. While he was on active service in the desert he was able to work through some of his feelings and his decision to concentrate on his political beliefs is an understandable reaction to his disillusionment in the sphere of love. It is only quite recently that *Dàin do*

Eimhir has been assessed as a complete cycle of love lyrics
and it may be that the delicate situation with the Scottish
'Eimhir' was one of the main reasons for MacLean's tendency
to try to disguise specific poems and identities. Certain poems
were moved from *Dàin do Eimhir* to the *Dàin Eile/Other
Poems* section of the 1943 edition and others were withheld
from publication altogether because they were judged as
being too personal. In later collections, such as *Reothairt
is Contraigh/ Spring tide and Neap tide* and *O Choille gu
Bearradh/ From Wood to Ridge*, poems belonging to *Dàin do
Eimhir* were given their own titles and were presented out
of sequence in different sections of the books. Although Iain
Crichton Smith's edition of *Dàin do Eimhir*, entitled *Poems
to Eimhir*, was published in 1971 and showed signs of seeing
it as a sequence in its own right, it was not until Christopher
Whyte's seminal edition was first published by the ASLS
in 2002 that *Dàin do Eimhir* could really be assessed as a
cycle of poems in its most complete form (with the excep-
tion of one poem which has not been found in the archives).
Whyte's edition succeeded in placing *Dàin do Eimhir* within
a proper context and chronological framework. In many
ways the conception and publication history of *Dàin do
Eimhir* is a perfect example of the various issues and argu-
ments surrounding the authorial right to conceive and then
re-write one's own literary-biographical history. From *Dàin
do Eimhir* questions arise such as the extent to which poetry
should be viewed as 'fact' in relation to a poet's private life,
the importance of structure within a sequence of poems and
the postmodern matter of the 'Death of the Author'.

While it is clear that the basis for many of these poems was
specific events and experiences in MacLean's life, a number
of these poems take these experiences and use them as a
catalyst to produce a poetry which embraces concepts such as
the eternal. In many of the poems in the collection the figure
of Eimhir is lifted out of the present and the imagery which is
employed is far more divine in nature – it would not be out of
place in a description of a goddess or heavenly being. In *Dàin
do Eimhir* LII galactic imagery is used to describe Eimhir's

beauty: 'Do m' dhùr amharc bha thu 'nad reul/ To my steady gaze you were a star' (pp. 154–155), while in *Dàin do Eimhir* LIV his love is given the attributes of the sun at dawn:

Bu tu camhanaich air a' Chuilithionn
's latha suilbhir air a' Chlàraich,
grian air a h-uilinn anns an òr-shruth
agus ròs geal bristeadh fàire.

You were dawn on the Cuillin
and benign day on the Clarach,
the sun on his elbow in the golden stream
and the white rose that breaks the horizon.
(pp. 156–157)

It is interesting to note that in many instances Eimhir's face is the main image used to describe his love and her beauty. For example, in *Dàin do Eimhir* XVII MacLean writes that there is no miracle but in love, 'soillse cruinne an lasadh t' aodainn./ lighting of a universe in the kindling of your face.' (pp. 16–17) and in 'An Tathaich/ The Haunting' (LVII) (pp. 158–164) it is Eimhir's face which haunts him as opposed to the complete form of a woman in his imagination. This vision of a face, almost disembodied in many of the poems, is not just a symbol of the woman's outer beauty. Eimhir's face seems to become the site from which her whole spirit shines forth – a refreshing change from the almost clichéd image of the eyes being a gateway to the soul – and it provides a calmness and serenity in opposition to the wrongs and injustices of mankind in *Dàin do Eimhir* XXIII:

An cuirear gu cuimir suas
anns a' chochur cluaineis saoghail,
ànradh an duine mhòir 's an truaigh
agus ciùin luathghair t' aodainn?

Will one neatly set up
in the synthesis the world's deceit,

the distress of the great and of the wretched,
and the mild paean of your face?
(pp. 24–25)

It is clear that the beauty that MacLean writes about in
relation to Eimhir's face is more than just skin deep. As also
happens in parts of 'An Cuilithionn', the corporal and the
spiritual aspects of a person intermingle as MacLean strives
towards the hope of transcendence. Christopher Whyte has
also pointed out that this coupling of the beautiful face and
soul is also evidence of MacLean's Platonism which theorises
that the beauty of the body is formed by the beauty of the
soul.

As a young poet who was greatly moved by feelings of
admiration and love for a woman, and who had a groun-
ding in Classical, Metaphysical and Romantic influences,
MacLean began to explore his feelings on another level
and struggled with how to turn something fragile and
transient into something more permanent and everlast-
ing. Poems such as 'Coin is Madaidhean-allaidh/ Dogs and
Wolves' (XXIX), 'Samhlaidhean/ The Ghosts' (XXVIII),
and 'An Tathaich/ The Haunting' (LVII) explore the idea
of eternity and the preservation of beauty and love. The
genesis of these poems is particularly intriguing. MacLean
has written that at 'about 2 or 3 a.m. on Wednesday 20th
[December 1939] I got up out of bed and very quickly
wrote down 'Samhlaidhean' and 'Coin', of which, as far
as I remember, I have never changed one word from that
first writing down. It seems to me that I composed them
simultaneously in a troubled sleep.' Christopher Whyte
has rightly suggested that this is something akin to 'auto-
matic writing' and I think MacLean's account of how he
came to write these two poems is indicative of the all-
consuming effect that this particular poetic and personal
experience was having on the poet. In 'Coin is Madaidhean-
allaidh' MacLean's own unwritten poems are imagined as
dogs and wolves, chasing the deer, a symbol for Eimhir,
across the snow of eternity:

coin chiùine caothaich na bàrdachd,
madaidhean air tòir na h-àilleachd,
àilleachd an anama 's an aodainn,
fiadh geal thar bheann is raointean,
fiadh do bhòidhche ciùine gaolaich,
fiadhach gun sgur gun fhaochadh.

the mild mad dogs of poetry,
wolves in chase of beauty,
beauty of soul and face,
a white deer over hills and plains,
the deer of your gentle beloved beauty,
a hunt without halt, without respite.
(pp. 134–135)

The almost violent urgency is palpable in rhythm and imagery. The figure of Eimhir is unattainable but this does not stop MacLean from attempting to catch up with her – it is unclear whether he will fail because her love is unattainable to him physically or whether he means that he can never capture all of her beauty in a poem and thus the essence of his love will be lost over time. It is likely to be the latter explanation which is truer if 'An Tathaich' is taken into consideration in the same context:

'N uair chrìonas tasgadh gach cuimhne
a bheir gaol no smuain no suim dhuit,
an caill thu mealladh t' aonachd
's tu faoin gun chuimhn' ort?

Cha n-iarrainn-sa gu bràth dhut
aon bhiothbhuantachd do t' àilleachd
ach na liùbhradh slàn i
dìreach mar a tha i.

When the hoard of every memory decays
that will give you love or thought or care
will you lose the delight of your unity,
vain and forgotten?

For you I would never seek
any lastingness for your beauty
but what would render it complete
exactly as it is.
(pp. 160–161)

These two poems hint at a more platonic love for Eimhir
and appear to look at a time which is beyond the sequence
itself. While MacLean's main striving is for the preservation
of beauty in an almost abstract sense, the very act of attempting to do this indicates his belief not only in poetry but in
his own role as poet. In *Dàin do Eimhir* XXXI (which was
not included in *O Choille gu Bearradh* – page numbers given
here refer to Christopher Whyte's edition) MacLean hints at
an inner dialogue or rivalry that he has with the Gaelic poet,
William Ross (1762–1791) whose famous poem, 'Òran Eile',
was dedicated to Marion Ross. Although in reality William
Ross died of consumption, the more romantic story is that
he died of a broken heart. In MacLean's poem he imagines
a conversation between himself and Ross about their poems,
thus aligning himself with Gaelic poets who went before him
and consciously placing himself in a significant place within
the wider Gaelic tradition:

Uilleim Rois, dè chanamaid
a' coinneachadh taobh thall a' bhàis?
Dhèanainn luaidh air t' Òran Eile;
dè theireadh tusa mu na dàin
a sgaoil mi ealain-shriante,
eachraidh fhiadhaich bhàrd.

William Ross, what should we say
meeting beyond death?
I should mention your 'Òran Eile'.
What would you say about the poems
I let loose art-bridled,
a wild cavalry for bards?
(pp. 86–87)

It is likely that MacLean's poetic relationship with Eimhir is a reciprocal one in a literary sense at least. In return for the poetic inspiration that Eimhir provides, MacLean gives her the gift of eternity, ensuring that her beauty and spirit exist in his poetry long after any physical aspect of 'Eimhir' has diminished. It could be argued that this relationship has undertones of the relationship which existed between the bard and chief in Gaelic tradition (the bard and chief relationship was reciprocal because each needed the other's talent and patronage to function in society) and also of the poetry of the troubadours who immortalised the object of their admiration. In this way MacLean's poetry succeeds in spanning the Gaelic and European traditions while also achieving something thoroughly personal and modern.

Conclusion and Further Reading

Dàin do Eimhir succeeds in capturing a specific period in the life of Sorley MacLean while also providing a blueprint of themes for other poems which he was yet to compose – the role of the poet, the concept of eternity, polarity and transcendence are all present in *Dàin do Eimhir* and, when later poems such as 'Nighean is Seann Orain/ A Girl and Old Songs' (pp. 224–227) and 'Iadhshlat/ Honeysuckle' (pp. 302–303) are surveyed in relation to MacLean's earlier work, it is clear that MacLean's 'Gaelic Muse', in her many guises, has always exercised a powerful effect on his poetry.

I have provided a short introduction to *Dàin do Eimhir* in this chapter, highlighting some of the main details and themes. However, if you are interested in reading more about the complete cycle the main source for study is Christopher Whyte's edition of the poems.

Notes

1. See Douglas Sealy, 'Out from Skye to the World: Literature, History and the Poet' in *Sorley MacLean: Critical Essays* ed. by Raymond J. Ross and Joy Hendry (Edinburgh: Scottish Academic Press, 1986) pp. 53–79 (p. 67). The English translation of this traditional song is by Christopher Whyte.

2. SORLEY MACLEAN'S POETRY OF CONSCIENCE: 'BAN-GHÀIDHEAL/ HIGHLAND WOMAN' AND 'CALBHARAIGH/ CALVARY'

It is perhaps an injustice to the rest of Sorley MacLean's work to pick out only a few of his poems and discuss them in the context of the poet's conscience when the great majority of his poems, including many of *Dàin do Eimhir* and his longer poems such as 'An Cuilithionn', have at their heart the theme of injustice and suffering and his approaches to this from his own perspective as a Gaelic poet and a self-proclaimed communist. However, it is in 'Ban-Ghàidheal/ Highland Woman' and 'Calbharaigh/ Calvary' that we can view MacLean's attitude towards social injustice in its most concentrated form, especially in relation to his often discordant feelings towards religion and its interaction with his socialist beliefs. While 'Ban-Ghàidheal' explores the hardship suffered particularly by the Gaels, 'Calbharaigh' has an urban setting. Both poems were included in the *Dàin Eile* section of *Dàin do Eimhir* (1943) and as such, provide a balance between his love lyrics and the more overtly socio-political verse. The *Dàin Eile* section often includes, but is not restricted to, landscape poetry as well as poems which explore his socio-political concerns, including Highland history and its effect on the present time. As well as the two poems which will be analysed in detail in this chapter, other significant poems include 'An t-Eilean/ The Island' (pp. 56–59) which is both a love lyric and a lament for Skye and its condition, 'Clann Ghill-Eain/ The Clan MacLean'(pp. 46–47) which calls for his clan to take pride in the Scottish socialist leader, John Maclean, in precedence to their traditional clan history, and 'Cornford' (pp.44–45), in which MacLean addresses his concerns for Spain and the wider implications for mankind.

Before discussing 'Ban-Ghàidheal' and 'Calbharaigh' in detail it is necessary to put them into context with MacLean's views regarding the Church since both poems often overtly reproach the church system. While it has been noticed by scholars such as John MacInnes that MacLean's poetic style is often influenced by evangelical sermons and the psalms, and many of his images of self-sacrifice and suffering have Christian reference points, MacLean was, nevertheless, at odds with the Christian tradition he was brought up within on Raasay. In what is now an often quoted statement, he wrote to Douglas Young in September 1941 that

> I was never a 'converted' seceder who had experienced 'conviction of sin, repentance into life, effectual calling, justification, adoption and sanctification' ... I was merely a child 'adherent', frequently experiencing what the Seceders call 'slavish fear' of the literal burning pit. So Portree school only confirmed a sort of anti-Secederism latent in my childhood ... Yes, my Promethean view of Socialism is an inversion of the career of the 'saved' in the sense that it was a justification of the 'lost', 'damned' Promethean.

'Secederism' is another name for the Free Presbyterian Church. In his essay 'My Relationship with the Muse' MacLean expands on this attitude towards 'Secederism' when he writes 'the odds for eternal damnation were terribly high against a very high percentage of the lovable people one knew. The obvious fewness of the Elect made me anti-elitist in most ways.' The Free Presbyterian Church believed that secular arts were dangerous vanities and that even the bulk of Free Presbyterians would suffer eternal damnation. For MacLean, who was greatly influenced by socialism, before, during and after the 1930s, the Free Presbyterian belief system was in direct opposition to his communist ideals. Much of his poetry dealt with this conflict, often in spite of his worries that some of it would upset his parents who were 'lax' Free Presbyterians, but who would still be affected by their son's public dismissal of the Church. However, MacLean's unfavourable view of Free Presbyterianism is not two-dimensional – he writes that 'in the Thirties I used to be very sceptical of the Scottish writers who seemed to attribute most of Scotland's ills to Calvinism. What did they know of Calvinism? Not one of them had been brought up in a small island where nine out of ten of the people were adherents of the Free Presbyterian and the

rest of the Free Church.' Other Gaelic poets, who had had the
same experience as MacLean, were voicing critical attitudes
towards the religion they had grown up with in the 1940s and
beyond. Iain Crichton Smith directly tackled the issue of the
role of the Church in Highland communities in poetry as well
as in his prose (e.g. his novel *Consider the Lilies*) voicing the
belief that ministers often did little to help their congrega-
tions and often sided with the landowners during events such
as the Highland Clearances.

'Ban-Ghàidheal/ Highland Woman' was composed in 1937
or early 1938. It is a poem of seven stanzas with four lines to
each stanza. In the first five stanzas MacLean describes the
appearance of the woman and the dismal nature of her existence and directly addresses Jesus Christ as he does this:

> Am faca Tu i, Iùdhaich mhòir,
> ri 'n abrar Aon Mhac Dhè?
> Am fac' thu 'coltas air Do thriall
> ri strì an fhìon-lios chèin?

> *Hast Thou seen her, great Jew,*
> *who art called the One Son of God?*
> *Hast Thou seen on Thy way the like of her*
> *labouring in the distant vineyard?*
> (pp. 26–27)

This first stanza alone is controversial because of the impli-
cation that MacLean is reproving Christ by asking if Christ
has seen the highland woman, implying that God is not all-
seeing or at least, that, if God has seen the woman's plight,
no hope has been given to her. This accusation is reinforced
in the third stanza in which MacLean writes 'Chan fhaca Tu
i, Mhic an t-saoir/ Thou hast not seen her, Son of the carpen-
ter' (pp. 28–29). The language which MacLean employs is
ecclesiastical in tone and style but this is undermined by the
emphasis on 'ri 'n abrar/ who art called' in the first and the
third stanza. In a religious context, this style of phrase is not
unusual in itself but, in the context of this poem in which the
poet is less than reverent to the Christian faith, it also subtly

leads the reader to assume that this belief in Christ's true identity is not necessarily held by the poet himself.

In contrast to the ambivalent picture of Christ, the second stanza succeeds in forming a very potent image of the highland woman as a figure of suffering:

An cuallach mhiosan air a druim,
fallus searbh air mala is gruaidh;
's a' mhias chreadha trom air cùl
a cinn chrùibte bhochd thruaigh.

The load of fruits on her back,
a bitter sweat on brow and cheek,
and the clay basin heavy on the back
of her bent poor wretched head.
(pp. 28–29)

The depiction of this woman almost renders her an icon herself – a martyred figure which would not be out of place as a painting or stained glass window. The emphasis on the martyred aspect of the woman is not an accident since it effectively compares her suffering to the suffering of Christ, who is the definitive figure of sacrifice and suffering. Of course, the highland woman refers not to a specific person but is a symbol which encapsulates what MacLean views as the suffering of the whole of the population of the Highlands and Islands. This is clear from the way MacLean describes her as a figure spanning many years:

An t-earrach seo agus seo chaidh
's gach fichead earrach bho 'n an tùs
tharruing ise 'n fheamainn fhuar
chum biadh a cloinne 's duais an tùir.

This Spring and last Spring
and every twenty Springs from the beginning,
she has carried the cold seaweed
for her children's food and the castle's reward.
(pp. 28–29)

The perpetual motion of the changing seasons and the work of the woman suggest that she is not alone and that this situation has been perpetuated in many different areas of the Highlands over time. She is also unnamed and so may stand for many who are in the same predicament. It is significant that it is a woman who is described in the poem. Firstly, she acts as a contrast to Christ in terms of gender and, when one considers Christ's compassion for women who suffered hardship in the Bible, it is fitting that this is the image set out by the poet. Secondly, other Gaelic poets, including Derick Thomson and Iain Crichton Smith, have employed the image of the highland woman in their poetry. It is entirely possible that what can be witnessed here is a more general 20th century Gaelic preoccupation with the symbolic 'mother' since the mother-tongue of Gaelic is in decline and many Gaels are also separated from the motherland due to emigration or social and spiritual dislocation. Links can also be made between this 20th century Gaelic woman's plight and the women in distress in the Irish aisling/ dream poems of the 17th century, in which male poets created the image of a woman as a symbol of Ireland who was suffering great hardship and was awaiting a saviour in the form of the Stuart Pretender. The difference in MacLean's poem is that he sets out no obvious saviour for the highland woman, despite addressing the poem to Christ. He offers the reader no sense of hope because he believes that the woman can have no hope in her own life as long as society continues unchanged – 'Is thriall a tìm mar shnighe dubh/ And her time has gone like a black sludge' (pp. 28–29). This black sludge is described as seeping through the thatch on her home and brings to mind the symbol of the morass in 'An Cuilithionn/ The Cuillin', which will be explored in more detail in Chapter 3. There the black sludge symbolises capitalism and all that is evil, swallowing up everything in its path, so it is very fitting that this symbol is also employed in this poem. After all, it is capitalism which MacLean believes is partly responsible for the plight of the highland woman, while the Church turns a blind eye. The image of black sludge seeping into every corner of life and obliterating hope is doubly evil because it also succeeds in removing the evidence of injustice from the eyes of the world and thus evil deeds are not remembered. This may be another reason why the highland woman remains unnamed. In MacLean's view, one of the roles of the poet is to bring attention to injustice, hence the repeated question to Christ of whether he can see the highland woman.

It is less likely that MacLean is remonstrating against the actual figure of Christ and far more likely that he is actually opposing the Free Church's doctrine when he writes in the sixth stanza: 'Agus labhair T' eaglais chaomh/mu staid chaillte a h-anama thruaigh; / And Thy gentle church has spoken/about the lost state of her miserable soul' (pp. 28–29). MacLean's real contempt is reserved for a belief system which does not even offer a poor woman the promise of a more joyous afterlife, never mind a slightly better standard of life in her present existence. MacLean's communist principles can be easily detected here. The poet is no stranger to the concept of sacrifice and injustice from an idealistic standpoint (he certainly revels in the ideal self-sacrificial hero – a concept which will be explored further in Chapter 4) but he is clearly portraying the realistic side of suffering in this poem. In other words, he is drawing attention to the people who have no choice in their lives and whose suffering does not lift them up beyond the 'everyday' to the heights of heroism and self awareness as named figures such as James Connolly achieve in some of MacLean's other poems.

MacLean continues this point in 'Calbharaigh', which was composed in November or December 1939, when he writes:

Chan eil mo shùil air Calbharaigh
no air Betlehem an àigh

*My eye is not on Calvary
nor on Bethlehem the Blessed*
(pp. 34–35)

Instead, the poet's attention is on the slums of Glasgow and Edinburgh, where poverty and pain exist and 'far bheil

an lobhadh fàis,/ where life rots as it grows' (pp. 34–35).
There are many levels to this statement. Firstly, MacLean is
exhibiting a very socialist concern with the here and now as
opposed to the past. Secondly, this poem could be viewed as
yet another slight against the Church since MacLean is effectively saying he is more concerned with the lives of ordinary
people than the trials of Christ within a Biblical setting.
However, on another level, MacLean may also be implying
that the suffering of the unnamed is of more importance
to him than that of well known Christ-like heroic figures
who can act as saviours to mankind. He stated in a letter
to Douglas Young in October 1940 that 'Christ and Lenin to
me are only almost random examples of great minds realis-
ing emotionally as well as intellectually the "miseries that
will not let them rest"'. It can, therefore, be assumed that
MacLean had no problem with Christ as a compassionate
figure of sacrifice, albeit as a figure existing for him outside
a Church framework, yet in 'Calbharaigh' he seems to reject
this. This dichotomy is a main theme in MacLean's work and
he often struggles with his need to record the suffering of the
masses while also holding up heroic martyred figures as the
ideal against the encroaching morass or black sludge which
destroys individuality.

Conclusion and Further Reading
In both 'Ban-Ghàidheal' and 'Calbharaigh' the sympathy
for the masses wins out against his admiration for an individual, heroic aesthetic but MacLean was evidently aware
of the opposing factors in his work and, in the early 1940s
after becoming disillusioned with his love for 'Eimhir' and
his search for a heroic self-identity in relation to his harness-
ing of the Muse, he wrote to Douglas Young that his next
poems would be more like 'Calbharaigh' and 'Ban-Ghàidheal',
presumably because he wanted to concentrate more on his
socialist concerns. This movement between the 'people's
poet' as spokesman for the masses and the idealistic poet,
concerned with the struggle for a more individual goal of
heroic self-identity, is something which MacLean explores in
many of his poems. 'Ban-Ghàidheal' and 'Calbharaigh' can

be viewed as examples of poems in which MacLean is at his most conscientious in relation to the wider concerns of the world.

Other poems with some relevance to his poems of conscience discussed above include 'An Crann Dubh' (pp. 36–37), another of the *Dàin Eile*, with images of Christ's cross which "s e spiacadh cridhe na h-Eòrpa/ has been spiking Europe's heart'. 'An Cuilithionn/ The Cuillin' has very clear links with some of the issues raised in this chapter and will be discussed in its own right in Chapter 3. A later poem 'Tìodhlacadh sa Chlachan/ Funeral in Clachan' is also relevant to MacLean's struggle with the belief system of the Free Presbyterian Church. It paints a grim picture of a funeral service for a Raasayman who was 'teò-chridheach, onorach is càirdeil/ warm-hearted, honourable and friendly' (pp. 236–237) but, like many of the people MacLean knew, he had little hope of eternal life according to Free Presbyterian doctrine because presumably he was not a true adherent of the faith. The only difference between this poem and MacLean's discussions about religion in his letters to Douglas Young is that the conclusion is in poetic form:

> Agus thuig gach fear sa chòmhlan
> nì nach seanaiseadh e ri ònrachd:
>
> nach eil trian de thrian a' creidsinn
> ann an Ifrinn bhuan na h-aidmheil.
>
> *Almost all the company understood*
> *a thing that one would not whisper to himself alone:*
>
> *that not a third of a third believed*
> *in the lasting Hell of their creed.*
> (pp. 238–239)

However, for a slightly more ambivalent example of a poem which employs imagery connected to the Church see 'Eaglais Chatharra/ A Church Militant' (pp. 300–301), which is included in the '1972 and After' section of *O Choille gu*

Bearradh. The church militant "na cheann/ in his head' is presumably a facet of the poet's own self.

For a more detailed discussion of the religious influence on MacLean's poetic style see John MacInnes, 'A Radically Traditional Voice: Sorley MacLean and the Evangelical Background' in *Dùthchas nan Gàidheal: Selected Essays of John MacInnes* ed. by Michael Newton, Edinburgh: Birlinn, 2006 pp. 381–391. In the same book there is also an essay, 'Religion in Gaelic Society' (pp. 425–442) which, while it does not refer specifically to Sorley MacLean, does elaborate on the development of the Free Presbyterian Church, thus providing a useful context for MacLean's poetry and themes.

3. STRIVING FOR THE HEIGHTS OF THE SELF – POLITICAL COMMITMENT AND 'AN CUILITHIONN/ THE CUILLIN'

Sorley MacLean called his long epic poem 'the rant', and he certainly does take every opportunity to berate many people and sections of society within 'An Cuilithionn/ The Cuillin' for the wrongs committed against mankind. 'An Cuilithionn' is definitely his most political poem and is also the one in which his communist ideals are at their strongest. He began this poem in 1939. During the time he held a teaching position on Mull, he became obsessed with the effects of the Clearances on the society and on the landscape around him. This depressed MacLean on a personal level because Mull is MacLean clan territory and thus MacLean realised that it was his own ancestors who had been deeply affected by the Clearances on this island. However, 'An Cuilithionn' is not just a Clearance poem – it is much more than that and operates on many levels. It would also be too simplistic to dismiss it as just a political poem in contrast to the more heartfelt love lyrics of *Dàin do Eimhir* since both 'An Cuilithionn' and many of the *Eimhir* poems were composed around the same time and they clearly influence and inform each other with their use of imagery and symbolism.

While there can be no doubt that MacLean's Gaelic tradition and sense of place affected the course that this poem takes, Hugh MacDiarmid's influence can also be seen. MacLean greatly admired 'A Drunk Man Looks at the Thistle' and it was his plan to try to emulate this epic structure with a long poem, interspersed with lyrical passages and 'lyric peaks' – those parts in which a climax or high point is reached both structurally and symbolically.

The mountain is a multi-facetted symbol within 'An Cuilithionn'. MacLean returns to the symbol of the mountain in many of his other poems – see for example 'A' Bheinn air Chall/ The Lost Mountain' (pp. 260–263), 'Creag Dallaig' (pp. 240–241) and 'Tìm is Sgùrr Urain/ Time and Sgurr Urain' (pp. 250–255). In 'An Cuilithionn', the mountain is a symbol

35

of fertility, polarity, and a witness of the wrongs of mankind. It is described as having horns or antlers and is envisaged as a boat and as a building with battlements. In one specific stanza in Part V, it is imagined as a number of creatures:

> Chithear an Cuilithionn
> 'na iolair iomaluath,
> 'na leòmhann suilbhir,
> 'na bheithir dheirg;

> *The Cuillin will be seen*
> *a multi-swift eagle,*
> *an affable lion,*
> *a red dragon.*
> (pp. 100–101)

In this sense, the mountain symbol is reminiscent of MacDiarmid's symbol of the thistle, which also takes on a multitude of meanings. The ever-changing symbol of the mountain provides the poem with a modernist context while also reinforcing the bond between the poet and his land-scape. In this short study of 'An Cuilithionn' I will specifi-cally concentrate on the symbols and images which MacLean employs in order to establish his sense of self and explore his identity in the poem in relation to both politics and Gaelic tradition and innovation.

A Brief Overview of 'An Cuilithionn'
'An Cuilithionn' is split into seven parts with a short introduc-tion before Part I, in which MacLean dedicates the poem to the 18th century Gaelic poet, Alasdair Mac Mhaighstir Alasdair (Alexander McDonald), and Hugh MacDiarmid, thus showing from the outset the influence of both tradition and modern-ism on his poetry. In many ways, 'An Cuilithionn' is his epic attempt at creating a space where both these aspects of his own personality can exist together. In Part I he praises the peaks of 'An Cuilithionn', showing how each one has a differ-ent character. The voice in the poem begins to ascend the

mountain and he sees visions of Skye poets who are long dead, such as Màiri Mhòr (Mary MacPherson) and Neil MacLeod. However, while he admires the beauty of his landscape, the 'villains' of Skye appear and take their places on the Cuillin peaks, looking down at what they have done to the landscape. Ghosts of lawyers, factors and landowners begin a macabre dance, celebrating their deeds and overshadowing Skye heroes of the Land Reforms, and the Cuillin cries out in agony. In Part II the voice in the poem seems to have an initiation of sorts with the mountain as mother/lover. He laments the state of Scotland and compares the local injustices with the struggles of the Republicans in the Spanish Civil War. In Part III the Morass of Mararabhlainn (an actual landscape feature at the foot of the Cuillin) is described as a bourgeois bog, which swallows up all of the beauty and heroism of the world as it moves and spreads over many countries. The poet wishes for the strength of Hugh MacDiarmid and the Skye poets of the past who would speak out against injustice. As a contrast to the evil morass, the summit of the Cuillin is described as a place where heroism of many different sorts (symbolised through the figures of Christ and Lenin) can exist side by side. In Part IV the morass is explored from a personal perspective, with MacLean fearing that it will drown his own spirit and heart. The whole tone of the poem changes in Part V with one of its most significant 'lyrical peaks'. The Skye Stallion (which is actually a rock formation of Waternish cliff in the north end of Skye) comes to life and leaps from peak to peak of the Cuillin, smashing the structures of capitalist society and trampling the bog. This section ends with MacLean's translation into Gaelic of MacDiarmid's 'If there are bounds to any man' from *Second Hymn to Lenin*. In Part VI the voice of the poet gives way to other voices – the girl from Gesto, a fictional figure from Skye, recounts her homesickness for her land after being sold into slavery and taken to America, and then the voice of Clio, the Muse of History, takes over and lists the heroes and villains of Skye, the Highlands and Scotland, before looking out towards Europe and the rest of the world, recounting the struggles of mankind throughout history. This is an important aspect of the poem, because it shows MacLean's sense of place

in the world: he begins by looking inwards at his own land
but then moves out to survey the whole world. In Part VII
figures associated with self sacrifice (Christ, Spartacus and
Prometheus) are seen as visions on the mountain peaks and
the mountain becomes the site of acts of heroism – in a surrealist fashion Marx, Lenin, James Connolly, Georgi Dimitrov
and other (often communist) heroes of the poet are seen alive
together and in the one place. The shouts of liberty can be
heard and the Cuillin is seen rising on the other side of sorrow.
In part VII the poet's experience on the mountain becomes
highly personal, with him seeing a spirit or 'journeying one'
who walks alone on the mountain a little away from the poet.
It may very well be the essence of the poet's own spirit and,
while he gets close to it, he never quite manages to reach it.
This spirit is always a little ahead of him. The poem ends with
the poet longing for the rising Cuillin.

Politics and Issues of Self-Identity in 'An Cuilithionn'
'An Cuilithionn' fell out of favour with MacLean and this
was the main reason for its delayed publication and heavy
editing. MacLean writes in his short introduction to the
poem in *O Choille gu Bearradh: Collected Poems* that 'the
behaviour of the Russian Government to the Polish insur-
rection in 1944 made me politically as well as aesthetically
disgusted with most of it. I reprint here what I think toler-
able of it.' MacLean's admiration for the Soviet Union is
difficult to ignore in the poem, with MacLean wishing for
the Red Army to come across Europe:

'S gus an tig an t-Arm Dearg còmhla
le caismeachd tarsainn na Roinn-Eòrpa,
drùidhidh iorram na truaighe
air mo chridhe 's air mo bhuadhan.

And until the whole Red Army comes
battle-marching across Europe,
that song of wretchedness will seep
into my heart and my senses.
(pp. 74–75)

With the benefit of hindsight, MacLean realised that communism was not always the 'hero' in the story but we would lose a significant portion of MacLean's poetry if we relegated 'An Cuilithionn' to the dusty shelf of history because of its now unfashionable political context. It is clear that there are heavy communist overtones in the poem. The mixing of the image of a sunrise with the communist red banner is one example of this:

> Chuala mi gum facas bristeadh
> agus clisgeadh air an fhàire,
> gum facas ròs dearg ùrail
> thar saoghal brùite màbte

> *I heard that a breaking was seen*
> *and a startling on the horizon,*
> *that there was seen a fresh red rose*
> *over a bruised maimed world*
> (pp. 96–97)

MacLean looks to communism for hope for humanity and even his religious image of self-sacrifice in the form of Christ is given a socialist slant:

> bha ioma biatach dè am Breatainn
> a rinn an obair oillteil sgreataidh,
> agus cheusadh ioma Crìosda
> an uiridh agus am bliadhna.

> *there were many god-vultures in Britain*
> *who did the loathsome hateful work,*
> *and many a Christ has been crucified*
> *last year and this year.*
> (pp. 120–121)

However, while 'An Cuilithionn' is rich in communist symbolism, the poem can also be read as MacLean's own search for hope, heroism and identity within himself. In the early sections of the poem MacLean enters into a very

intimate relationship with his own landscape as he describes
his ascent of the Cuillin:

A Chuilithinn chreagaich an uamhais,
tha thusa mar rium dh'aindeoin fuathais,
...
a' cheud là phòg mi do bhial
dh'fhosgail Iutharn a dhà ghiall;
a' cheud là laigh mi air d' uchd-sa
ar leam gum faca mi an luchdadh
aig na speuran troma, falbhaidh
gu crith sgriosail na talmhainn.

Rocky terrible Cuillin,
you are with me in spite of life's horror.
...
the first day I kissed your mouth
hell opened its two jaws;
the first day I lay on your breast
I thought I saw the loading
of the heavy swift skies
for the destructive shaking of the earth.
(pp. 76–77)

In this description the reader is given the sense of the
Cuillin's sublime nature and the awe MacLean feels as he
climbs its slopes. MacLean has written that he spent many
of his days as a young man climbing the Cuillin ridge and the
early sections of 'An Cuilithionn' certainly contain elements
of the personal experience of a climber interacting with his
environment. From the Cuillin peaks MacLean figuratively
surveys his whole world and the mountaintop gives him a
clear vision of reality as he sees it – not only do the injustices
of mankind and the threat of fascism weigh heavily upon
him but also the sense of his role as poet or spokesman of the
people. This is especially clear in Part III when he worries
that the morass has seeped into his own soul and he feels
the presence of the 19th century Skye poet, Màiri Mhòr, at
his side:

Ach chan inns mi dh' a spiorad làidir
nach tàinig tilleadh air an tràigh ud;
seachnaidh mi clàr treun a h-aodainn
's mo sgeul air buaidh ar n-Eilein traoighte.

But I will not tell her strong spirit
that no turning has come on that ebb-tide
I will avoid her brave forehead,
as my tale is of the ethos of our island ebbed.
(pp. 90–91)

MacLean's personal sense of duty to his land makes him feel uncomfortable in the gaze of poets who have gone before him. Of course, the gaze of these poets is an imagined one, conjured up by MacLean himself, but the responsibility he feels is no less valid for him. Comparisons can be drawn between this feeling of the weight of tradition from a Gaelic perspective and the modernist concern with the influence of earlier poets, which is best encapsulated by T.S. Eliot in his famous essay 'Tradition and the Individual Talent'.

One of the main symbols in the poem, the Skye Stallion, is also inextricably bound up with MacLean's own emotional ties to his island, his people and his hope for the future of mankind. The rising of the Stallion comes directly after his personal fears about the morass overpowering him, and while the Stallion is an entity separate from the poet, he nevertheless uses the energy and power generated from this creature to build up and sustain his own power. When he writes

Siod ort fhèin, Aigich lùthmhoir,
prannaidh tu bùirdeasachd nam fùidsean,
ni thu sìnteag thar na mointich;
chan eil thu tuilleadh air an òtraich:
chan eil thu nis 'nad thruaghan gearrain;
chaill na boglaichean am mealladh.

Here's to you, mighty Stallion,
you will pound and smash the pimps' bourgeoisie,
you will career across the morass;

you are no longer on the dung-heap;
you are no more a poor gelding;
the swamps have lost their wiles.
(pp. 96–99)

it is difficult to separate his hopes for the emergence of
communism from his hopes that his own political 'impotence'
will also be cured in the process – his use of MacDiarmid's
'If there are bounds to any man' hints at his poetic and philosophical striving for something just beyond his grasp and
this theme is returned to at the end of the poem with the
'journeying one'. 'Tannasg eanchainne luime nochdte/ The
ghost of a bare naked brain' and 'an samhla a chunnaic an
t-anam,/ the ghost seen by the soul' (pp. 128–129) suggest
that the poet is glimpsing a highly personal vision here.
Throughout the poem MacLean appears to struggle with the
separate parts of his own self, namely his intellect and his
heart/spirit. While his admiration for Lenin's intellect may
be at odds with Christ's heroic self-sacrifice, these figures
become examples of mankind's potential and the mountaintop is the site where the meeting of mind and heart becomes
achievable:

chan fhaicear an dithis còmhla
a dh'aindeoin farsaingeachd na mòintich;
chan fhaicear ann an aon àit' iad
ach air mullach lom nan àrd bheann.

The two may not be seen together
for all the expanse of the morass;
they are not to be seen in one place
except on the bare tops of the high mountains.
(pp. 90–91)

Despite the multitude of voices in the poem and the abun-
dance of heroic figures, these voices and figures eventually
merge into one vision and it is clear that this is deliberate.
MacLean may praise Dimitrov, Connolly and others in 'An
Cuilithionn' for their socialist principles but it is their heroic

spirit and sense of self-sacrifice that the poet is really striving towards. By naming these people as his heroes MacLean is trying to catch a glimpse of his own heroism and what he himself is capable of and he almost succeeds in the last stanzas of the poem with the vision of the 'journeying one'. It is enough to glimpse this journeying spirit on the Cuillin and know that this is the goal even if complete synthesis of mind and spirit is unattainable. It may be that it is MacLean's own journey towards self identity on the Cuillin that is most significant.

'An Cuilithionn' is rich in symbolism and imagery which have connections to many of his other poems; it can be viewed as a part of a greater poetic process, a personal journey for the poet rather than a detached study of the predicament of mankind. A woman bearing a resemblance to 'Eimhir' makes an appearance in Part VII of the poem:

> Chaidh mo ghaol liom air a' bheinn
> fiach an cluinneadh i an t-seinn
> a bha air stùcan nan ceum gàbhaidh;
> chual is leth-thuig i 'm mànran
> agus air ball bha cruth na biataich
> air a bhòidhche ghil chianail
> agus 's ann tholl i mo chliathaich.

> *My love went with me on the mountain*
> *so that she might hear the singing*
> *on the peaks of the dangerous steps;*
> *she heard and half understood their melody,*
> *and at once the form of the vulture*
> *took her fair sad beauty*
> *and she holed my body.*
> (pp. 122–123)

It may be that the poet's love does not share his hatred of fascism or does not hold his communist principles and therefore he feels betrayed by her – in *Dàin do Eimhir*, the Irish 'Eimhir', as a pious Catholic, is thought by MacLean to be conservative in politics and thus sympathetic to Franco in the

Spanish Civil War. (See *Dàin do Eimhir* VIII, pp. 10–11, which
is especially pertinent to this section of 'An Cuilithionn'). As
well as connections to Eimhir, other parallels can be drawn
between the girl from Gesto in Part VI of 'An Cuilithionn'
and MacLean's earlier poem, 'Ban-Ghàidheal'. The traditional story of the Gesto girl is that she was kidnapped
and sold into slavery in America and, when approached by
a Highlander in the King's army who asked her the time,
she spoke to him in Gaelic, saying, 'am crodhadh chaorach
mu dhà thaobh Beinn Dubhagraich/ It is the time one folds
the sheep on the two slopes of Ben Duagraich'. Compare the
Gesto girl's plight:

> Dh'fhuiling mi daorsa nan stràc,
> an dubh-chosnadh is grian le àin
> a shearg m' fheòil air mo chnàmhan
> 's a rinn creachadh air a' bhlàth òg
> a bha 'na mo ghruaidhean 's 'nam aodann

> *I suffered slavery with strokes*
> *the 'black labour' and a sun with a heat*
> *that withered my flesh on my bones*
> *and harried the bloom of youth*
> *that was on my cheeks and forehead*
> (pp. 104–105)

with the woman in 'Ban-Ghàidheal':

> 'S gach fichead foghar tha air triall
> chaill i samhradh buidh nam blàth;
> is threabh an dubh-chosnadh an clais
> tarsuinn mìnead ghil a clàir.

> *And every twenty Autumns gone*
> *she has lost the golden summer of her bloom;*
> *and the Black Labour has ploughed the furrow*
> *across the white smoothness of her forehead.*
> (pp. 28–29)

MacLean's sympathy for these women is apparent but his sense of injustice on their behalf goes beyond mere pity. In his poetry, their suffering and feelings of hopelessness and abandonment become pure emotion which seeps into the landscape. It is this emotion in 'An Cuilithionn' which causes the crying out and shaking of the mountain, as it feels the plight of its people. This cry could be connected to the lyrical cry of the 'old songs' in Gaelic tradition, of which MacLean is so fond. The girl from Gesto's homesickness and longing for her mother's house and Beinn Dubhagraich is reminiscent of these old songs and it is fitting that the Gesto girl's voice then gives way to a strophic form used by 17ᵗʰ century poets such as Mary MacLeod, in keeping with this theme of praise of the landscape:

> am Minginis
> as grinne slios,
> as guirme pris, mo rùn;
>
> an Eilean Sgitheanach
> nam beann sgiamhach,
> nam monadh riabhach,
> mo chiall 's mo smaoin;
>
> *In Minginish*
> *of the most lovely slopes,*
> *of the greenest bushes, my love.*
>
> *In the Island of Skye*
> *of the beautiful hills,*
> *of the brindled moors,*
> *my delight and thought;*
> (pp. 108–109)

Comparisons can be drawn between 'An Cuilithionn's' range of different voices and other modernist poems such as T.S. Eliot's 'The Wasteland'. However, unlike the situation in Eliot's poem, there is an underlying sense of hope

in 'An Cuilithionn', despite MacLean often stating that he
views himself as a pessimistic poet. While Modernism is
often characterised by shifting and unstable identities, it
must be remembered that MacLean, as a Gaelic poet, had a
much firmer sense of his history and identity because he was
part of a well-established tradition. His poetry thus reflects
a certain amount of confidence despite his feelings of inse-
curity and worry for the future of Europe, which was facing
the threat of fascism. Symbols such as the Stallion, the Gesto
girl and the figure of Màiri Mhòr do not just provide him with
reference points within a real and poetic landscape; they also
embody the actual landscape. By making his chief symbol
the Cuillin, on which visions come to him as almost tangible
forces, he is able to gain the confidence and strength to look
out towards the rest of the world because his feet are firmly
placed on the rocks of his own land.

Conclusion and Further Reading
While the myriad of voices such as the Gesto girl and the heroes
on the Cuillin are connected, both symbolically and emotionally, to the landscape, they also form a relationship with the
poet himself. 'An Cuilithionn' can be viewed as a quest for
identity for MacLean. Every aspect of the poem is an exploration of the personal and its place within the collective. From
the mountain, MacLean can figuratively 'see' the rest of the
world but he can only do this because he is firmly anchored to
what he knows so well. The ascent of the Cuillin could be used
as an analogy for MacLean's own growing understanding of
his sense of heroism, but he must fight against the sickness
of the morass which will swallow up his individuality and
his personal heroic strength, very much like the silent threat
of capitalism and fascism which was seeping into the unconscious of many people at this time. Thus, MacLean's personal
struggles are effectively acted out using landscape symbols
and a modern Gaelic poetry begins to emerge from the older
tradition which has such a rich history of song and poetry
with the image of the mountain as its backdrop and often
as its main subject. (The 18th century Gaelic poet Duncan
Ban MacIntyre's 'Moladh Beinn Dòbhrain/ In Praise of Ben

Dorain' is a good example of the use of mountain imagery and makes a good starting point for those who want to view how MacLean has moved the tradition forward.) Until MacLean's poetry, the landscape, which held a great deal of importance to the Gaels in relation to hunting, clan and cultural identity, had never been so thoroughly identified as a signifier of the self but with the emergence of psychoanalytical theory it was perhaps to be expected that a modern poet such as MacLean would reassess the landscape in light of these ideas.

I hope this brief introduction to 'An Cuilithionn' has proved that, while politics feature in the poem in so far as the political context informs MacLean's personality and sense of self, it has deeper levels of meaning. 'An Cuilithionn' was very much 'of its time' but it also contains possibilities beyond it. The concepts of heroism, hope and idealism are universal in scope, and MacLean's belief in these concepts was unwavering beyond any of the beliefs he held about the Soviet Union around the late 1930s.

For other poems by MacLean which contain symbolism closely linked to MacLean's self-identification with his own native land see 'An Coilltean Ratharsair/ The Woods of Raasay' (pp. 170–183) which was written at approximately the same period as 'An Cuillithionn'. This poem has at its centre the symbol of the wood and there is definitely a case for studying the polar opposites of the woods of Raasay and the Cuillin which would have been visible to him from his home on Raasay. While the summit of the Cuillin provides the poet with a clear view outwards and a sense of striving, the wood is more 'inward' in scope and is filled with images relating to his unconscious drives and creativity. See also the later poem, 'Eadh is Fèin is Sàr-Fhèin/ Id, Ego and Super-Ego' (pp. 242–245) for an overt reference to Freud and psychoanalysis.

4. A GAEL IN THE DESERT – SORLEY MACLEAN'S WAR POEMS

On 26th September 1940 MacLean left Edinburgh for military training at Catterick Camp in Yorkshire and in December 1941 he was sent to Egypt on active service as a member of the Signal Corps. After MacLean was wounded at the Battle of El Alamein in November 1942 he had to recover in military hospital and was eventually discharged from Raigmore Hospital, Inverness, in August 1943.

Although it could be argued that Sorley MacLean composed many poems on the theme of war throughout his lifetime, he has a small number of published poems under the heading of 'Blàr/ Battlefield' in *O Choille gu Bearradh* that have become known specifically as his war poems because they deal with his personal experiences during World War II. These poems are very valuable to Scotland, and indeed, Britain's, corpus of WWII war poetry because they add an important dimension to this period as the voice of a Scotsman and Gael.

When approaching MacLean's war poems it is probably best to view them as interconnected with the greater whole of his work rather than a separate entity. MacLean has written that he was 'not a pure conscript' and anyone expecting to read poems describing experiences of war from a British-centric perspective will be disappointed. MacLean chose to become a soldier because of his deep-seated loathing of fascism but he also wanted to remain true to his communist principles and often struggled with the choice he had made. Joining the British army did not always sit well with him. While he was in training and then during his time abroad on active service, he wrote many long letters to his friend, Douglas Young, who was resisting conscription for nationalist reasons and these letters become a way of comprehending his stance in relation to communism.

One of Maclean's most straightforward war poems is 'Alasdair MacLeòid', in which he shows an appreciation for his Gaelic tradition in the form of an elegy of two stanzas to a friend from Raasay, who had been lost from the RAF in 1942. There is emphasis on MacLeod's clan ancestry and the description of MacLeod's character could have come straight from an 18th century Gaelic poem:

fhir mhisneachail mheanmnaich
's tu cho còir agus uasal,
cho dàna is dealbhach.

spirited courageous one,
so kind and generous,
so daring and handsome.
(pp. 206–207)

It is likely that MacLean employed a traditional style for his lost friend (and presumably for the benefit of Alasdair MacLeod's family too) because this style and form would be well understood by Gaels familiar with these conventions and was thus both a recognition of his own Gaelic tradition and the most respectful way in which MacLean could honour a fellow Gael.

Other war poems are more complex in scope. In one poem, 'Dol an Iar/ Going Westwards', he gives the impression that the war enabled him to put into perspective the personal experiences which he describes in *Dàin do Eimhir*, removing him from his previous situation and providing distance between him and his failed love affair – 'fada bhuam 'san Aird an Iarthuath/ na sùilean glas-ghorma 's bòidhche/ far from me in the North-West/ the most beautiful grey-blue eyes' (pp. 204–205). The last stanza is particularly ambivalent in tone. Is he determined to march headlong into battle because of, or in spite of, his wounded heart? However, it is clear that he cannot (and will not) lose his own sense of self. Despite having no rancour towards the enemy because they are all just men 'am prìosan air sgeir-thràghad/ in prison on a tidal rock' (pp. 204–205), in the last stanza of the poem he lists his clan connections and their corresponding attributes. He asks 'cò bu trèine/ nuair dh'fhadadh uabhar an lèirchreach? / who were braver/ when their ruinous pride was kindled?' (pp. 206–207). As the first poem in the section 'Blàr/ Battlefield', 'Dol an Iar' is well placed to show

MacLean looking back at what had gone before and then turning to his future and the task in hand in the desert. In this poem MacLean is asserting that first and foremost, he is a Gael. His pride may have been hurt in matters of the heart and his attitude to the men fighting for the enemy may be ultimately more benevolent than would be expected but he will not let this affect him in the throes of battle because he will retain the characteristics of his ancestors. This poem is also a perfect introduction to the disorientation and, to a certain extent, the emptiness which he must have felt on foreign soil, away from his familiar landscape. His homesickness is also homesickness for everything he once held certain and which is now being shaken by the reality of participation in the war:

'S fhada bhuam-sa an t-Eilean
agus gach ìomhaigh ghaoil an Alba,
tha gainmheach choigreach anns an Eachdraidh
a' milleadh innealan na h-eanchainn.

Far from me the Island
and every loved image in Scotland,
there is a foreign sand in History
spoiling the machines of the mind.
(pp. 204–205)

Can it be that his moral and political sensibilities are being unsettled as the war unfolds? *Dàin do Eimhir* and 'An Cuilithionn' were the poems he had written before being conscripted and, while the war poems chart new territory in the sense that these are new experiences for MacLean, the way he processes these experiences and the philosophical approach he takes is not far from his political and moral stance in poems such as 'Ban-Ghàidheal', 'Calbharaigh' and 'An Cuilithionn'. If anything, the main development is that the hypothetical quandaries MacLean places before himself in earlier poems suddenly become much more real and immediate when he faces the human aspect of fascism while in combat.

In particular, MacLean's poem 'Glac a' Bhàis/ Death Valley' shows this development of thought and experience. In the poem MacLean remembers a German soldier, whom he refers to as a boy, and describes his feelings when he found him dead below the Ruweisat Ridge. The poem begins with a quote:

'Thubhairt Nàsach air choireigin gun tug am Furair air ais do fhir na Gearmailte "a' chòir agus an sonas bàs fhaotainn anns an àraich".'

'Some Nazi or other has said that the Fuehrer had restored to German manhood the "right and joy of dying in battle".'
(pp. 210–211)

The poem is effectively an answer to these lines and illustrates the reality of Hitler's Nazi regime in which many young men joined because of the promise of glory:

Smaoinich mi air a' chòir 's an àgh
a fhuair e bho Fhurair,
bhith tuiteam ann an raon an àir
gun èirigh tuilleadh;

I thought of the right and the joy
that he got from his Fuehrer,
of falling in the field of slaughter
to rise no more;
(pp. 212–213)

MacLean deliberately highlights the grim reality of injury and death on the battlefield:

le cuileagan mu chuirp ghlas'
air gainmhich lachduinn
's i salach-bhuidhe 's làn de raip
's de sprùidhlich catha.

with flies about grey corpses
on a dun sand

dirty yellow and full of the rubbish
and fragments of battle.
(pp. 212–213)

However, the poem has another facet and becomes a meditation on the injustice of war in general. The genesis of this
poem is discussed by MacLean in a letter to Douglas Young
dated 27th October 1942 in which he writes:

> The first dead man I saw in action was a young German
> sitting in a pathetic attitude in a dugout entrance. He
> made me ashamed of many foolish generalisations I had
> often made about the necessity of wiping out all Fascists.
> Probably he wasn't a Fascist at all, or, if he was, only of the
> kind the ordinary politically unconscious man must be in
> every Fascist country ...

We can glean from this letter that it is highly likely
MacLean's experience of seeing his first dead man in action
influenced his thoughts greatly and thus inspired 'Ghlac a'
Bhàis' but MacLean also takes this experience and uses it
to explore his political ideals. There can be no doubt that
this dead German has forced MacLean to deal with familiar
labels such as 'fascism' in more detail – a dead soldier
certainly humanises the face of the enemy. While he questions whether this boy abused Jews and communists some
sympathy begins to creep into the poem in the latter stanzas
when he wonders if the boy was of the band of those

a threòraicheadh bho thoiseach àl
gun deòin gu buaireadh
agus bruaillean cuthaich gach blàir
air sgàth uachdaran?

led, from the beginning of generations,
unwillingly to the trial
and mad delirium of every war
for the sake of rulers?
(pp. 212–213)

The mention of rulers here hints at the fact that MacLean has not abandoned his communist beliefs and that, in fact, they are actually strengthened by his experiences. In some ways this poem is not just anti-fascist but is also anti-imperialist since the poet recognises that soldiers such as himself and the dead German are one and the same. They can be viewed as cogs in the wheel of a power struggle between rulers. He looks past his sense of heroic idealism and, death making all men equal, he redefines his political parameters.

This is not the only poem in which MacLean's sense of sympathy lies with the common man, irrespective of political and national boundaries. In 'Curaidhean/ Heroes' MacLean writes about an English soldier – 'Fear beag truagh le gruaidhean pluiceach/ A poor little chap with chubby cheeks' (pp. 208–209) – who showed great bravery and was killed in battle. In contrast to 'Alasdair MacLeòid', this poem places tradition in second place to innovation. It is highly likely that this soldier was also based on a real man or even a number of real men. From the outset it is clear that, while this poem praises the hero's bravery, it is not composed in the form of a traditional Gaelic praise poem in which the chief or hero is described as superior in appearance and accomplished in the deeds he carries out. On the contrary, 'Curaidhean' is MacLean's answer to traditional Gaelic praise poetry straight from the horrifying landscape of modern battle. The subverting of traditional poetic devices thus becomes a way of accentuating the modern predicament. Firstly, the specific hero described in the poem is not attractive like the Gaelic heroes described in praise poetry – 'aodann guireanach gun tlachd ann/ pimply unattractive face' (pp. 208–209) – but MacLean makes it clear that this does not hinder his courage. His face is 'còmhdach an spioraid bu trèine/ garment of the bravest spirit' (pp. 208–209). The third stanza develops this theme:

Cha robh buaidh air ''san tigh-òsda
'n àm nan dòrn a bhith 'gan dùnadh,'
ach leòghann e ri uchd a' chatha,
anns na frasan guineach mùgach.

He was not a hit 'in the pub
in the time of the fists being closed,'
but a lion against the breast of battle,
in the morose wounding showers.
(pp. 208–209)

The reference in lines one and two of this stanza has
been lifted from an older Gaelic praise poem about Allan
MacDonald of Kingsburgh, Skye, who was being attacked
by members of the Martin family and who showed physical
prowess in this situation. Again, the man in MacLean's
poem does not exhibit the attributes so often expected by a
traditional ceilidh-house audience. Nevertheless the hero
is described as 'lion-like' despite not being a conventional
hero. Everything in the poem is described in exceptionally
realistic terms. Rather than a long drawn out act of heroism
before the hero is killed, the man's life is snuffed out quickly
(Stanza 5) and his death is distinctly ugly rather than beau-
tifully tragic:

gus an d'fhuair e fhèin mu 'n stamaig
an deannal ud a chuir ri làr e,
bial sìos an gainmhich 's an greabhal
gun diog o ghuth caol grànda.

until he himself got, about the stomach,
that biff that put him to the ground,
mouth down in sand and gravel,
without a chirp from his ugly high-pitched voice.
(pp. 210–211)

While MacLean is not turning his back on his established
perceptions of heroism, the devices he is familiar with from the
bardic tradition and the old songs are deliberately subverted
in order to underline the real human sacrifice behind the
heroism. Although only one man is described in the poem,
the plural 'heroes' of the title shows that MacLean is aware
that this is not an isolated case and that many brave individuals are needed to make the existence of heroism a reality

and not just a romanticised concept. It is interesting to note that MacLean is following the same themes that subtly underpin 'Glac a' Bhàis' when he mentions that this fallen soldier in 'Curaidhean' would gain no posthumous medal and few of his comrades would have lived to vouch for his bravery either. In the line "'s nan robh cha bhiodh am facal làidir/ and if there were their word would not be strong' (pp. 210–211). MacLean hints at the expendable nature of the troops who were playing their part within a larger situation that they had no say in. This soldier was one of the 'masses' so close to MacLean's heart. The first stanza of the poem is also evidence of MacLean's communist principles which were foremost in his mind as this point in his life:

Chan fhaca mi Lannes aig Ratasbon
no MacGill-Fhinnein aig Allt Eire
no Gill-Iosa aig Cuil-Lodair
ach chunnaic mi Sasannach 'san Eiphit.

I did not see Lannes at Ratisbon
nor MacLennan at Auldearn
nor Gillies MacBain at Culloden,
but I saw an Englishman in Egypt.
(pp. 208–209)

While MacLean shows an awareness of the Gaelic tradition of naming heroes, the man in this poem is not named and he is one of many if the plural title is to be taken into consideration in this context. Gaelic poetry has never shied away from listing a long roll-call of heroes but this is a very different kind of war from the battles experienced by clans in which family loyalty and ancestry played an important part. MacLean is showing the nature of the war he is fighting and how impersonal death has become. In this poem the lack of named heroes does not make the fallen soldiers any less worthy in MacLean's mind. It is also important that MacLean states that the soldier is an Englishman. Again, this does not fit the convention of Highland heroes in Gaelic praise poetry and elegies but MacLean's experiences in the barracks during his army training and then his friendship with the soldiers he was fighting alongside had put him in contact with English privates of whom he spoke highly in his letters to Douglas Young. 'Curaidhean' shows that heroism can be found in the unlikeliest of places, irrespective of nationality, and is certainly not exclusive to well-known and important Gaelic figures. However, it is perhaps fitting that the last line of the poem, 'is thug e gal beag air mo shùilean/ and he took a little weeping to my eyes' echoes the concluding line of the elegy for Alasdair of Glengarry by his relative, Sìleas na Ceapaich, which she composed after his death around 1720. He was a Jacobite who had fought at Sheriffmuir and many elegies have been composed for him, this one by Sìleas being one of the most famous. The English soldier and the great Alasdair of Glengarry are effectively aligned by MacLean in this poem, ensuring that MacLean's message is emphasised. It should also be noted that MacLean is usually keen on naming his heroes such as James Connolly, Lenin and Dimitrov in other poems in the same way that Gaelic poets from previous centuries would name their clan chiefs and heroes such as Alsadair of Glengarry. However, in 'Curaidhean' he balances his view of heroism by concentrating on the collective aspect of heroism, which would have been a natural direction for him to take during a period when he was experiencing the loss of a number of his comrades on a weekly basis.

Conclusion
MacLean's war poetry offers a firsthand insight into the mind of not only a Gael, but also an 'impure' conscript who is torn between his need to fight fascism and his communist principles. His honest tendency to show this conflict in his poems is largely unique in WWII poetry and represents yet another facet of his work. To a certain extent, his poetry is thematically chronological because his war poetry is the final result of the years of his philosophical predicament during the Spanish Civil War in which he struggled with his self-proclaimed inaction. By the time of the 'war poems' the reader can glimpse the final result of this struggle and how the realities of his war experience affect MacLean's heroic sensibility.

5. A RESURGENCE OF NATURE AND POETRY – 'HALLAIG'

Hallaig is a township north of Beinn na Lice on the island of Raasay which was cleared after 1846. In 1846 the island was purchased from Mac Ghille Chaluim by George Rainy, a son of a Highland minister and of a notable Highland family. This was the year of the potato famine but Rainy's attitude to the poor people of Raasay was not charitable – emigration, in some cases forced, was his answer to the situation. Fourteen townships were cleared by Rainy on Raasay, including those mentioned by MacLean in 'Hallaig'– Suisnish, Leac, Fearns, Screapadal, and Hallaig itself.

Out of all the stand alone poems which Sorley MacLean composed during his life, 'Hallaig' could be described as the one which has had the greatest impact on Gael and non-Gael alike. Douglas Sealy has written that 'if MacLean had written nothing but 'Hallaig' his claim to fame would be secure.' It is a magical, haunting poem and has succeeded in influencing many poets and artists. The musician and composer, Martyn Bennett, set a sound recording of MacLean reading 'Hallaig' in both English and Gaelic, to music, and this piece of music has become famous in its own right for the way the music and words merge (much like the way in which music and lyric have often mingled and become one entity in the Gaelic tradition). Seumas Heaney composed his own translation in English of 'Hallaig' in 2002 and Martyn Bennett's 'Hallaig' was used as an accompaniment to Neil Kempsell's short film, also entitled 'Hallaig', which used flash and digital layering combined with traditional drawn sequences in order to provide a visual medium for the poem.

On one level 'Hallaig' is a poem about the Highland Clearances from the perspective of a 20th century Gaelic poet. MacLean personally experienced the effect of the Clearances on the Gaelic psyche while still retaining a sense of the present and future. Because of this well balanced perspective, it is a far more hopeful poem than the 19th century Gaelic poetry of the Clearances in which the poets were often too close to provide non-sentimental accounts of events.

57

'Hallaig' begins with the line 'Tha tìm, am fiadh, an
coille Hallaig/ Time, the deer, is in the wood of Hallaig' (pp.
226–227). This line hints at the theme of the whole poem
– that time is a living entity which exists in Hallaig and,
by extension, the poet's own consciousness. The first stanza
proper begins with the now legendary lines:

Tha bùird is tàirnean air an uinneig
troimh 'm faca mi an Aird an Iar.

The window is nailed and boarded
through which I saw the West.
(pp. 226–227)

This evocative image of a boarded up, abandoned house
becomes a symbol of the Clearances as a whole. The entire
'West' – the Highlands and Islands – can be surveyed through
this window. It is a window into the very soul of the Gaels and
their experience of loss and desolation. However, the mood
changes almost immediately as the birch tree and the poet's
love become one and the same. MacLean never elaborates
on who his love is. She may be his Muse, a figure not unlike
Eimhir from his earlier poems, or a symbol of the spirit of the
Gael such as the Gesto girl from 'An Cuilithionn' or another
aspect of 'Ban-Ghàidheal/ Highland Woman':

's tha mo ghaol aig Allt Hallaig
'na craoibh bheithe, 's bha i riamh

eadar an t-Inbhir 's Poll a' Bhainne,
thall 's a bhos mu Bhaile-Chùirn:
tha i 'na beithe, 'na calltuinn,
'na caorunn dhìreach sheang ùir.

and my love is at the Burn of Hallaig
a birch tree, and she has always been

between Inver and Milk Hollow,
here and there about Baile-chuirn:

she is a birch, a hazel,
a straight, slender young rowan.
(pp. 226–227)

The birch tree is often the first species of tree to repopulate a deserted and arid area and thus can be viewed as a symbol of recovery and regeneration.

In stanza 3 MacLean personalises the poem by emphasising that it was his own people who lived in Screapadal:

Ann an Screapadal mo chinnidh,
far robh Tarmad 's Eachann Mòr,
tha 'n nigheanan 's am mic 'nan coille
a' gabhail suas ri taobh an lòin.

In Screapadal of my people
where Norman and Big Hector were,
their daughters and their sons are a wood
going up beside the stream.
(pp. 226–227)

This sense of ownership, of pride in belonging, is reminiscent of his war poem 'Dol an Iar', in which he proudly asserts his lineage:

tha mi de dh'fhir mhòr' a' Bhràighe,
de Chloinn Mhic Ghille Chaluim threubhaich.

I am of the big men of Braes,
of the heroic Raasay MacLeods.
(pp. 206–207)

His mention of particular ancestors such as Tarmad and Eachann Mòr in such familiar terms in 'Hallaig' disrupts the sense of linear time, as these long-dead men become part of the present, adding to the importance and weight of history. In terms of history, 'Hallaig' can be interpreted in a variety of ways. MacLean's mention of individuals and place-names adds to the idea that Hallaig is both a symbol and an embodiment of a humanised Gaelic landscape which is both tragic and redemptive. It is tragic because of the real events of history: the people and places MacLean mentions in the poem are irrevocably altered by history. And yet MacLean's vision is also redemptive because, as an artist, his vision comes to life in front of his eyes despite the very real loss of people and culture:

Tha iad fhathast ann a Hallaig,
Clann Ghill-Eain's Clann MhicLeòid,
na bh' ann ri linn Mhic Ghille Chaluim:
chunnacas na mairbh beò.

They are still in Hallaig,
MacLeans and MacLeods,
all who were there in the time of Mac Gille Chaluim:
the dead have been seen alive.
(pp. 228–229)

Heaney points out that 'the land of the living and the land of the dead become pervious to each other, when the deserted present becomes populous with past lives.' The idea that trees are populating an area once populated by people should be a depressing vision and yet this image is not one of despair in 'Hallaig'. MacLean writes:

Fuirichidh mi ris a' bheithe
gus an tig i mach an Càrn,
gus am bi am bearradh uile
o Bheinn na Lice f' a sgàil.

I will wait for the birch wood
until it comes up by the cairn,
until the whole ridge from Beinn na Lice
will be under its shade.
(pp. 228–229)

The growth of a wood is organic and natural and perhaps this is the very essence of MacLean's hope for his own land

and people. He is willing to wait for this resurgence and, in this context, the emphasis on the merging of the sons and daughters of Raasay with native trees should not be underestimated. When MacLean writes

Uaibhreach a nochd na coilich ghiuthais
a' gairm air mullach Cnoc an Rà,
dìreach an druim ris a' ghealaich –
chan iadsan coille mo ghràidh.

Proud tonight the pine cocks
crowing on the top of Cnoc an Ra,
straight their backs in the moonlight –
they are not the wood I love.
(pp. 226–229)

he is setting in opposition the non-native trees against the familiar native birch, rowan and hazel of Raasay. It is tempting to view the pine cocks and conifers as the landowners and the enemies of the islanders. The practice of equating vegetation with people is not unusual in Gaelic poetry. The older panegyric poetry of the medieval Bardic tradition often used trees to describe the strength, nobility and beauty of the chief of a clan or the clan or family tree itself. The native trees in 'Hallaig' are invested with the same sort of dignity the people of that area would have had in the old praise poetry. Thus, MacLean is creating links with the Gaelic past and using metaphors which embed his modern themes within a greater overarching tradition.

Perhaps the sense of hope that something remains within the land springs not only from this continuity of tradition but also from the sense of movement which is inherent throughout the whole of 'Hallaig'. The birch wood moves up by the cairn, and as the poet goes down to Hallaig he witnesses the girls coming and going:

's na h-igheanan 'nam badan sàmhach
a' dol a Chlachan mar o thùs.

Agus a' tilleadh as a' Chlachan,
à Suidhisnis 's à tir nam beò;
[...]
O Allt na Feàrnaibh gus an fhaoilinn
tha soilleir an dìomhaireachd nam beann
chan eil ach coimhthional nan nighean
a' cumail na coiseachd gun cheann.

and the girls in silent bands
go to Clachan as in the beginning.

and return from Clachan,
from Suisnish and the land of the living;
[...]
From the Burn of Fearns to the raised beach
that is clear in the mystery of the hills,
there is only the congregation of the girls
keeping up the endless walk.
(pp. 228–229)

The break between stanzas of the girls going to Clachan
and then returning is particularly effective in showing the
passage of time. This perpetual motion between the land of
the living and the land of the dead takes place at twilight
– 'anns a' chamhanaich bhalbh bheò/ in the dumb living
twilight' (pp. 228–229). The twilight in 'Hallaig' is not the
Romantic Celtic Twilight about which MacLean has voiced
his frustrations regarding its irrelevance to authentic Gaelic
tradition. Here MacLean may be using 'twilight' deliberately
in this context to present us with a more authentic 'Gaelic'
twilight. It is at this time of day that the world becomes
blurred and time gives way to timelessness. This blurring
of the edges is developed further in the second last stanza of
the poem when the girls' beauty clouds the poet's vision and
the landscape darkens as night draws in:

's am bòidhche 'na sgleò air mo chridhe
mun tig an ciaradh air na caoil.

and their beauty a film on my heart
before the dimness comes on the kyles.
(pp. 230–231)

The sense of timelessness which can be felt within the landscape prepares the way for the climax of the poem:

thig peileir dian à gunna Ghaoil;

's buailear am fiadh a tha 'na thuaineal
a' snòtach nan làraichean feòir;
thig reothadh air a shùil 's a' choille:
chan fhaighear lorg air fhuil ri m' bheò.

a vehement bullet will come from the gun of Love;

and will strike the deer that goes dizzily,
sniffing at the grass-grown ruined homes;
his eye will freeze in the wood,
his blood will not be traced while I live.
(pp. 230–231)

In what is probably the most symbolic stanza of the whole poem, time is the deer which is being hunted by the gun of love. Time is brought down by the gun of love and thus time is stilled and the eternal takes over. This is done without bloodshed and this corner of the poet's own land and also his own imagination remains intact despite its tragic history. By stilling time and ending the linear movement of history the poet succeeds in preserving his sense of place and the emotion of the land itself. The absence of the cleared people loses the connotations of heartbreak when Hallaig takes on the mantle of an eternal mythopoeic landscape. The fact that the gun which freezes time is a gun of love is also pertinent to the overall theme because love and hope appear to conquer, at least for a time, the events such as the Clearances and emigration that the land has witnessed. The last stanza of the poem is not as subjective as the earlier parts – the

actual hunter is not mentioned but since this is a poem about
MacLean's own poetic landscape it is possible that the hunter
is MacLean himself and he is carrying out a similar role to
that in *Dàin do Eimhir* XXIX, 'Coin is Madaidhean-allaidh/
Dogs and Wolves', where his poems are described as wolves
in pursuit of the deer of beauty and inspiration. In 'Hallaig'
he is attempting to capture a moment in eternity.

'Hallaig' is steeped in imagery from Gaelic tradition. For
example, the deer and the hunter are motifs which have
often been used in Gaelic poetry throughout the centuries
and the motif of the tree in Gaelic poetry has already been
mentioned. However, it is also an inherently modern poem
and many of MacLean's major themes, which run through
all of his poetry, can be viewed in this one poem. Tensions
and contraries exist in 'Hallaig' as they do in many of his
other landscape poems, e.g. the gun, an instrument with
connotations of violence, is instead an embodiment of love;
the Sabbath of the dead is walked by figures who are very
much 'alive' to the poet. Nothing is as it seems in 'Hallaig'
and these touches add to the surreal mood of the poem.

Conclusion and Further Reading
Like many modernist poems, 'Hallaig' is universal in scope.
C.A. MacLellan has written that he remembers MacLean at
a poetry reading commenting that 'I am against Clearances
wherever they occur'. 'Clearances' is a symbol of something
worldwide and 'Hallaig' is a poem which strives to find the full
meaning of 'clearances' locally and further afield by engaging
both heart and intellect. In the modern age, when traditional
society often seems to be in a state of flux, the need to protect
a way of life despite the odds can be well understood. 'Hallaig'
was composed many years after the themes of hardship and
social injustice had been explored by MacLean in poems
such as 'An Cuilithionn', and also years after he had experi-
mented with concepts such as the preservation of beauty
and the eternal in *Dàin do Eimhir*. It is perhaps fitting that
despite his periods of disillusionment with love and politics,
as well as his experiences of war in North Africa, MacLean
once again found an uncanny sense of joy and hope within

his own landscape, which has always been the touchstone for his philosophical and poetic explorations.

The last poem included in *O Choille gu Bearradh* is 'Screapadal' (a township in North Raasay) (pp. 304–313) and, while it is a very different poem from the more visionary 'Hallaig', the history included in this poem acts as a good companion piece to some of the names and place-names mentioned in 'Hallaig', including mentions of the cleared townships and perpetrators of the Clearances such as Rainy.

6. MACLEAN'S SELF-SACRIFICIAL HERO IN IRELAND AND BEYOND

Sorley MacLean's personal heroes are referred to many times throughout his poetry and in this section two specific figures will be studied in a little more depth. It must be remembered that MacLean viewed himself as a Gael first and foremost and this identity included cultural links with Ireland as well as his personal ties with Scotland. Ireland was one of the first countries outside Scotland to recognise the importance of MacLean's poetry and his brother, Calum, dedicated many years of his life to researching folk culture in Ireland. Also, the connections between the Highland clans and Irish clans stretch back hundreds of years – the Jacobite struggle was a reality in Ireland as well as Scotland. All of these factors contribute to MacLean's affinity with Ireland.

These personal and cultural ties may be one reason why MacLean gives such a special place in his poetry to the Irish socialist leader, James Connolly. Connolly was born in Edinburgh in 1868 (thus the link between Ireland and Scotland is once more strengthened) and after arriving in Dublin in 1896 he helped found the Irish Socialist Republican Party. He co-founded the Irish Labour Party with James Larkin in 1912 and he strongly opposed the Allied war effort when war broke out in 1914. He was best known for being one of the leaders of the Easter Rising in Dublin in 1916. The revolt failed and he was executed for treason at Kilmainham Gaol, Dublin, by a British firing squad. Although at the time public support for the Rising was certainly not widespread in Ireland (it was not even widespread in Dublin), by the time the Easter rebels had been executed and those who had been imprisoned in England returned to Ireland, sympathy for their nationalist cause was growing and the leaders of the Rising became martyrs and symbolic of the Irish struggle against British rule in general. Their myth grew and put into motion events that would lead to eventual partition and independence from Britain (as well as the creation of Northern Ireland). This development was not ignored by people outside Ireland. In Scotland, many nationalists and socialists looked to Ireland as an example of what could be achieved and MacLean's friend, James Caird, notes that while 'Pearse [Patrick Pearse – another leader of the Rising] and Connolly played a prominent part' in the political discussions they had as students, it was James Connolly as a socialist who 'above all appealed to Sorley's imagination, an appeal that has lasted'.

MacLean refers to Connolly by name a number of times throughout his early poetry – he pays tribute to his bravery in the eighth stanza of *Dàin do Eimhir* XVIII and also in parts of 'An Cuilithionn'. However, it is in 'Ard-Mhusaeum na h-Eireann/ The National Museum of Ireland' where MacLean makes his most sustained tribute to Connolly. It is no surprise that MacLean focussed on Connolly since he was the most clearly defined socialist presence within a group of cultural and political nationalists, and was thus ideologically compatible with MacLean himself. This poem of 24 lines can be found in the 1945–72 section of MacLean's *O Choille gu Bearradh: Collected Poems* and centres on the image of Connolly's bloodstained shirt which he wore when he was executed and which the poet is now looking at in the National Museum of Ireland:

> cha d' rinn mise ach gum facas
> ann an Ard-Mhusaeum na h-Eireann
> spot mheirgeach ruadh na fala
> 's i caran salach air an lèinidh
> a bha aon uair air a' churaidh
> as docha leamsa dhiubh uile

> *I have done nothing but see*
> *in the National Museum of Ireland*
> *the rusty red spot of blood,*
> *rather dirty, on the shirt*
> *that was once on the hero*
> *who is dearest to me of them all*
> (pp. 258–259)

The shirt itself is given the same sort of reverence as someone else may give a holy relic and this attitude of almost religious veneration is continued throughout the remainder of the poem. MacLean shows how important Connolly is to him by stating that he was dearest to him of all those who stood against bullets, tanks, cavalry and bombs. Considering the number of personal heroes MacLean lists in poems such as 'An Cuilithionn' who were involved in armed struggles, this is a significant tribute to Connolly! One can only wonder if the first part of the poem hints at the reason for this tribute at this specific time in the early 1970s:

Anns na làithean dona seo
is seann leòn Uladh 'na ghaoid
lionnrachaidh 'n cridhe na h-Eòrpa
agus an cridhe gach Gàidheil
dh' an aithne gur h-e th' ann an Gàidheal,

In these evil days,
when the old wound of Ulster is a disease
suppurating in the heart of Europe
and in the heart of every Gael
who knows that he is a Gael,
(pp. 258–259)

The mention of the Troubles and the acute pain MacLean feels at these events *as a Gael* is significant. By the late 1960s and early 1970s the modern troubles in Northern Ireland had begun with widespread rioting, the Battle of the Bogside in Derry and Bloody Sunday being broadcast across the world. MacLean is showing his knowledge of the situation. The fact that he states it is an old wound shows that he understands the origins of what is currently happening, but it is perhaps the fact that the Troubles are taking place so near to home that makes MacLean so aware of his own Gaelic heritage. He feels inextricably bound to Ireland through his Gaelic blood and thus the events in Ireland affect him even more. He turns to his own heroes such as Connolly because it is perhaps easier to look to figures from further back who are not involved with present day controversial events. They are at a safer distance, while still being very much 'alive' in the poet's own mind. MacLean is at this stage looking to his heroes to strengthen his own belief that heroism is still a reality. Connolly is the perfect example of MacLean's own brand of heroism.

It was Connolly's socialism which drove him to stand with others at the General Post Office in 1916 but Connolly did not concentrate on myths, symbols and poetry to the same extent as his more nationalist comrades such as Patrick Pearse and Joseph Plunkett. W.B. Yeats asks the question 'Did that play of mine send out/ Certain men the English shot?' in his poem 'The Man and his Echo', in reference to his nationalist play *Cathleen ni Houlihan* (1902). Yeats realised that this play had affected and influenced many nationalists to the extent that they became politicised with some even taking part in the Rising years later. By asking this question in his poem, Yeats is effectively adding to the mythology of the Easter rebels and incorporating them into the Irish tapestry of literature and myth as well as acknowledging their more conventional place in history. While not ignoring Connolly's socialist stance and the realism of his struggle, MacLean nevertheless adds to this mythology in his own poem:

> an lèine bh' air O Conghaile
> ann an Ard-Phost-Oifis Eirinn
> 's e 'g ullachadh na h-ìobairt
> a chuir suas e fhèin air sèithir
> as naoimhe na 'n Lia Fàil
> th' air Cnoc na Teamhrach an Eirinn.

> *the shirt that was on Connolly*
> *in the General Post Office of Ireland*
> *while he was preparing the sacrifice*
> *that put himself up on a chair*
> *that is holier than the Lia Fail*
> *that is on the Hill of Tara in Ireland.*
> (pp. 258–259)

MacLean fuses images of the chair Connolly sat on to be executed (because of his injuries which had become gangre-

nous, he had difficulty standing) with the throne of Tara
which has ancient significance in relation to the crowning
of kings in Ireland. The underlying suggestion here from
the poet is that the socialist cause is more important, and
indeed 'holier', than the rite of coronation of Irish kings.
He plays with socialist and royal images in *Dàin do Eimhir*
too, and has referred to 'an t-aobhar naomh/ the holy cause'
in 'Cornford' (pp.44–45) in relation to the struggle against
fascism in Spain. Death for a cause such as this becomes
self-sacrificial, with overtones of heroic Christ-like surren-
dering of the self for the sake of the people and the renewal
of life. In Gaelic tradition the king would become married
to the land (the throne of Tara reference is thus pertinent
here) and with this sovereignty came responsibility and
the possibility of sacrifice. MacLean is therefore mythologising Connolly's death within a specifically Gaelic-centred
worldview.

The final few lines of the poem solidify Connolly's place in
MacLean's mythic-poetic landscape:

Tha an curaidh mòr fhathast
'na shuidhe air an t-sèithir,
a' cur a' chatha 's a' Phost-Oifis
's a' glanadh shràidean an Dùn-èideann.

The great hero is still
sitting on the chair,
fighting the battle in the Post Office
and cleaning streets in Edinburgh.
(pp. 258–259)

In MacLean's poem, Connolly's actions are not in the past
but instead can be viewed as being very much of the present.
The mention of him cleaning the streets in Edinburgh
refers to his early life in Edinburgh when the Irish immi-
grants who were housed in the slums of the Cowgate were
viewed with suspicion and condescension. MacLean's sense
of perpetuity rather than linear, historical time suggests
that Connolly's heroism is not bound up with mortality but

instead has far more potential within eternity. He is a living reality for the poet and this heroism can therefore be tapped into by MacLean when he is in need of hope and inspiration. MacLean's real tribute to Connolly is to give him immortality within his poetry, just as he does with 'Eimhir'.

MacLean's poem to W.B. Yeats, 'Aig Uaigh Yeats/ At Yeats's Grave', which is of the same period as his tribute to Connolly, is a more ambivalent poem. MacLean's attitude to Yeats changed many times over the years. While he freely admitted that Yeats had influenced some of *Dàin do Eimhir* and that in the early 1940s 'his poetry has become one of my obsessions', at other times he was less enthusiastic about him, writing to Hugh MacDiarmid in 1936 that Yeats was 'a man full of all sorts of misgivings and indecisions, making half-hearted attempts to make the best of a few worlds.' In 1940 in a letter to Douglas Young, MacLean exhibits more reservations about Yeats: '... most of his finest poetry is just a specious camouflage for his feelings ... I even doubt the depth of his feelings to Maud Gonne. After all he did not become a revolutionary for her sake. He just remained a crossed troubled aesthete.'

Much of MacLean's uneasiness with Yeats stems from MacLean's own view of himself and his role as a poet. W.B. Yeats influenced many Irish nationalists with his poetry and plays, but he himself did not participate in militant activity. Indeed, he came to the ultimate conclusion that political involvement led to fanaticism and hate and that it damaged many people he loved, including Maud Gonne and his friend, Constance Markievicz. Thus, Yeats found himself in the position of cataloguing the events in Ireland as a poet, but never participating in them. This choice between action and inaction was something MacLean grappled with and this comes through most clearly in *Dàin do Eimhir*. MacLean viewed with contempt the stance of poets such as the 17th century poet, Iain Lom, who saw it as his duty to praise those who fought rather than do the fighting himself. In this instance, the role of the bard does not sit well with MacLean. However, because of his own personal struggle with the choice between action and inaction, MacLean cannot completely discount Yeats's own position and by the time of 'Aig Uaigh Yeats' his position regarding the other poet is softer in its approach.

The poem begins with MacLean contemplating figures and images at a location in Ireland (much as he does in the National Museum of Ireland). He is at the foot of Ben Bulben where Yeats and his wife are buried but Ben Bulben also becomes the site of a multitude of images and poetic fragments in MacLean's mind. Yeats's own poem, 'On a Political Prisoner', which features Constance Markievicz is also set at Ben Bulben:

> ... long ago I saw her ride
> Under Ben Bulben to the meet,
> The beauty of her countryside

Like MacLean's 'An Cuilithionn', in which mythical and historical ghosts rise from many different periods of history and fragments of song and poetry are heard on the wind, Ben Bulben accommodates its fair share of cultural and poetic references. MacLean's one-way conversation with Yeats at the poet's grave gives MacLean a chance to praise the quality of the Irish poet's language but the poem also becomes a meditation on heroism. Constance Markievicz supported the revolutionary Labour cause and she was second-in-command of the detachment of James Connolly's Citizen Army at St Stephen's Green at Easter 1916. MacLean admires Markievicz's decision to act for what she believed in and he goes to considerable lengths in 'Aig Uaigh Yeats' to reverse some of the criticism levelled at her by Yeats in his poem 'Easter 1916'. Compare Yeats's words:

> That woman's days were spent
> In ignorant good-will,
> Her nights in argument
> Until her voice grew shrill.
> What voice more sweet than hers
> When, young and beautiful,
> She rode to harriers?

with MacLean's second stanza:

An guth binn air slios Beinn Ghulbain
o 'n aon bhial cuimir òg
a thug a chliù o Dhiarmad
on chualas e air Grìne,
's air fàs 'na sgread le bròn
agus leis an fheirg uasail
is leis na h-euchdan còire
bu bhinn an cluais O Conghaile
's an cluasan a sheòrsa.

The sweet voice on the side of Ben Bulben
from the one shapely young mouth
that took his fame from Dermid
since it was heard on a Green
become a screech with grief
and with the noble anger
and with the generous deeds
that were sweet in the ears of Connolly
and in the ears of his kind.
(pp. 260–261)

MacLean does not deny that her political involvement changed her but he elaborates on why this came to be and it is clear that he looks on her dedication to the socialist cause to be as pleasing to the likes of Connolly and himself as Yeats viewed her voice to be in her early days.

MacLean's tendency to look on his native landscape as a storehouse of history and oral tales is extended in this poem to include Irish soil. He mentions the legend of Diarmid and Gràinne. Diarmid was killed by an enchanted boar on Ben Bulben and MacLean once more employs myth to expand the socialist allusions in his poetry by putting Constance Markievicz's 'story' above Diarmid's. This is more significant than it might appear. Like the myths and stories associated with his own island, Diarmid's story is much loved and gives a sense of uniqueness and character to this area of Ireland. The fact that Markievicz is given more importance in MacLean's

poem shows his undeviating passion for his socialist principles. MacLean is aware of his role as a poet and his ability
to reshape and add to the storehouse of memory and culture
already in place within the landscape.

Having dealt with the ghosts and literary traces on Ben
Bulben, MacLean once more turns his attention to Yeats.
Rather than berate Yeats for his lack of action in comparison
to Connolly and Markievicz, as the younger MacLean might
have tended to do in the late 1930s and early 1940s, it is a
wiser and older poet's voice which comes through in the last
stanza:

> Fhuair thusa 'n cothrom, Uilleim,
> an cothrom dha do bhriathran,
> on bha a' ghaisge 's a' bhòidhche
> 's an croinn bhratach troimh do chliathaich.
> Ghabh thu riutha air aon dòigh,
> ach tha leisgeal air do bhilean,
> an leisgeal nach do mhill do bhàrdachd,
> oir tha a leisgeal aig gach duine.

> *You got the chance, William,*
> *the chance for your words,*
> *since courage and beauty*
> *had their flagpoles through your side.*
> *You acknowledged them in one way,*
> *but there is an excuse on your lips,*
> *the excuse that did not spoil your poetry,*
> *for every man has his excuse.*
> (pp. 260–261)

Yeats was surrounded by friends and acquaintances who
showed 'gaisge/courage' and bòidhche/beauty' – the beauty
MacLean has in mind here is the beauty of self-sacrifice and
the hope and regeneration that such deaths may bring. Yeats's
tendency to acknowledge these people but not to partake in
the same choices himself means that MacLean's one-way
conversation with Yeats becomes a conversation with himself.
Just as MacLean berates himself for doing nothing but look at

Connolly's shirt in 'Ard-Mhusaeum na h-Eireann', likewise, in 'Aig Uaigh Yeats', he acknowledges the quandary between words and action once more and, if he finds Yeats lacking, he finds himself lacking also. MacLean, as an older man and an older poet, has not lost his sense of idealism but he also understands that no decision is made easily and that, while the death of the figures he admires may seal their heroism, the 'leisgeal/excuse' is also a reality which must be given its place. By the end of the poem he has not resolved this dilemma but, nevertheless, he has acknowledged that this choice exists and perhaps this acknowledgement is sufficient.

Conclusion and Further Reading

I have chosen in this chapter to give a close reading of MacLean's symbol of the self-sacrificial hero with strong Irish links. While there can be no doubt that the Irish heroes were well understood by MacLean because of the shared Gaelic heritage of Ireland and Scotland, it must also be stressed that MacLean was equally at home (sometimes even more so) writing about heroes such as Lorca, Julian Bell and Cornford (see 'Cornford' pp. 44–47) in the context of the Spanish Civil War or Jan Palach during the political protests in the late 1960s after the Prague Spring (see 'Palach' pp. 244–247), as he was about traditional 'Gaelic' heroes. MacLean was always interested in unconventional heroes – unconventional in the sense that they were socialists who were ideologically far removed from long established heroic figures. In reality, Connolly was not a 'Gaelic' hero. He was anti-establishment and European in his outlook but MacLean exhibits a talent for rewriting the images and symbols of his tradition and incorporating new figures who make sense of his identity both as a socialist and a Gael. In one way, he is developing the tradition, much as his predecessors did during the Gaelic Land Agitation and Land Reforms of the 19th century, when poetry charted the protests and everyday heroism of the people. However, underlying MacLean's contemporary context is the sense that these heroes contain an essence greater than the sum of their parts – an essence which is imperative for the hope of mankind.

7. AFFIRMING THE TRADITION – 'CUMHA CHALUIM IAIN MHICGILL-EAIN/ ELEGY FOR CALUM I. MACLEAN'

'Cumha Chaluim Iain MhicGill-Eain/ Elegy for Calum I. MacLean' is a poem which Sorley MacLean composed to commemorate his brother, Calum, after his death in 1960. On one level it is an example of MacLean using his role as poet in a highly personal way, as a respectful exercise in a modern interpretation of traditional bardic praise for a close family member. In this sense the poem is not unlike his earlier poem, 'Alasdair MacLeòid', except that his poem to his own brother is much longer. The poem is divided into four parts and the length of the poem could be attributed simply to the closeness of the subject of the praise, and yet there are instances in the poem in which the main subject, Calum, becomes symbolic of something far more universal in the poet's mind. Like many Gaelic traditional praise poems, this poem is formulaic, with hints of much earlier panegyric in which the subject is praised for his courage and kindness and his death is lamented. However, MacLean also achieves a personal quality with reminiscences about the day he heard of his brother's death:

> 'N Di-màirt sin as a dheaghaidh
> thàinig Pàdraig leis an sgeul,
> le naidheachd a chunnaic mi 'na aodann.

> *On the Tuesday after*
> *Peter came with the tale,*
> *With news I saw in his face.*
> (pp. 274–275)

The personal aspect of the poem, particularly the dense number of place-names and people's names, means that while the subject matter is fairly simple compared to MacLean's more symbol-driven poetry, it is actually one of his more unapproachable poems, especially if the reader has little or no knowledge of folklore, the Highlands and Islands or the specific people involved. For example, in stanza 15, Donnchadh Peigh'nn an Aoirein refers to the story-teller, Duncan MacDonald of South Uist, and Dòmhnall Ruadh Phàislig or Dòmhnall Mac an t-Saoir/ Donald MacIntyre (1889–1964) from Snishival, South Uist, refers to a Gaelic poet who passed on many of the waulking songs, charms and other traditions to Calum MacLean and Dr John L. Campbell. Reference to these figures and others in itself ensures that, to a certain extent at least, 'Cumha Chaluim Iain MhicGill-Eain' remains a private poem for MacLean, despite the fact that it does not deal with the intimate inner workings of the poet himself in the way that the collection *Dàin do Eimhir* does. Perhaps this was a conscious effort on the part of MacLean as a way of honouring his brother and coming to terms with his own loss.

Calum MacLean (1915–1960) was a folklorist, ethnographer and collector, who took a first class degree in Celtic Studies at the University of Edinburgh (1935–1939) and went on to study Early Irish and Medieval and Modern Welsh at University College Dublin. He worked for the Irish Folklore Commission, collecting folklore in the Connaught Gaeltacht, before being sent to the Hebrides where he collected an immense amount of material in his native Raasay and in South Uist, Barra, Benbecula and throughout the mainland Highlands – the poem's impressive roll-call of place-names is indicative of how far and wide Calum MacLean travelled in his quest for folklore. He was an instrumental figure of the School of Scottish Studies founded in 1951 at Edinburgh University, where he became Senior Research Fellow. His use of modern recording apparatus was an important development in folklore collecting. In the late 1950s he suffered from cancer and he died in 1960 at the Sacred Heart Hospital, Daliburgh, South Uist. MacLean makes repetitive mentions of Cnoc Hàllainn/ Hallin Hill in the poem – Calum MacLean was buried at Hàllainn Cemetery, South Uist. He had very close connections with South Uist, claiming the island as his own and the people claiming him as one of their own. MacLean refers to this in stanzas 8 and 9:

O nach eil thu anns a' Chlachan
no air Cnoc an Rà
miosg nan Leathanach 's nan Leòdach,
dh'fhàg sinn thu a-miosg Chlann Dòmhnaill.
Chan eil àite 's fheàrr.

Miosg nan daoine treuna còire
tha thu anns an ùir:
on bu thoigh leinn riamh Clann Dòmhnaill
thug sinn dhaibh a' ghibht bu chòire
nuair chuir sinn thu 'nan ùir.

Since you are not in Clachan
or on Cnoc an Ra,
among the MacLeans and MacLeods,
we left you among Clan Donald.
There is no better place.

Among the brave generous people
you are in the dust.
Since we always liked Clan Donald
we gave them the most generous gift
when we put you in their dust.
(pp. 266–267)

These stanzas are particularly interesting because MacLean employs clan terminology in order to discuss the final resting place of his brother. It is difficult to tell whether MacLean is trying to explain why his brother was buried on South Uist rather than his birthplace of Skye because he is regretful of this himself and is thus working through this for his own benefit, or because he is at pains to explain the reason to others who were less conversant with Calum MacLean's life. Either way, MacLean reverts to mentions of clan connections as a way of explaining and rationalising this situation. In Part IV of the poem comparisons are again made between Skye and South Uist, with landscape symbols being employed rather than clans:

Dhìrich mi Dùn Cana
Di-haoine roimh do bhàs,
cha robh mo shùil ach air Uibhist
– cha b' ionnan 's mar a b' àist –
dhìochainich mi 'n Cuilithionn
's mo shùil air a' Bheinn Mhòir,
air Teacal is air Staolabhal.
'Sann dh'fhàs iad uile mòr.

I went up Dun Cana
on the Friday before your death,
my eye was only on Uist
– not as it used to be –
I forgot the Cuillin
looking at Ben More,
at Hecla and Staolaval.
They all grew big.
(pp. 274–275)

Note the comparison between MacLean's own personal landscape symbols of Dùn Cana on Raasay and the Cuillin on Skye, and the landmarks of South Uist which he associates with his brother – A' Bheinn Mhòir/Ben More (2033ft) and Teacal/Hecla (1988ft) dominate the eastern side of South Uist, while Staolabhal is also a mountain in South Uist. In many of MacLean's poems, in particular 'An Cuilithionn', the symbol of the mountain has very close connotations with the poet's own self and it is fitting that in this poem the mountains of these separate islands are not only used as landmarks but also as a way of illustrating how the poet has laid aside his own concerns for a time to concentrate on the state of his brother. Also, by mentioning the great mountains of South Uist in relation to his brother, MacLean succeeds in transferring the qualities of these mountains onto Calum, thus ensuring that the poem stays true to its original function as an elegy.

Throughout the poem MacLean makes mention of his brother's qualities using traditional methods in a modern

setting. This is clearly not an elegy for a heroic warrior or
clan chief but by describing Calum MacLean's exploits the
poet gives the same admiration to his subject. For example,
he associates the 'bravery' of his brother's tireless folklore
collecting in Scotland and beyond with the bravery of any
conventional clan hero:

Tha iomadh duine bochd an Albainn
dh' an tug thu togail agus cliù:
'sann a thog thu 'n t-iriosal
a chuir ar linn air chùl.
Thug iad dhutsa barrachd
na bheireadh iad do chàch
on thug thu dhaibh an dùrachd
bu ghrìosach fo do bhàidh.

There is many a poor man in Scotland
whose spirit and name you raised:
you lifted the humble
whom the age put aside.
They gave you more
than they would give to others
since you gave them the zeal
that was a fire beneath your kindness.
(pp. 266–267)

MacLean is alluding to his brother's ability to collect stories
and songs from people who may have found it difficult to
pass on their knowledge under circumstances where recording apparatus made them uncomfortable or nervous. This is
one of the most problematic aspects of folklore collecting and
is generally difficult to overcome. Calum MacLean's character and friendly manner with people clearly contributed to
his success in his work. MacLean's mention of many areas of
Scotland and beyond where Calum MacLean travelled with
his research, and the clan names which are connected to
these locations, are also used to show his strength of character. The stanza preceding Part III is particularly successful
in melding the past with the present:

Bha thu san Ros Mhuileach
mar Leathanach nach trèigeadh,
mar Eachann Bacach air tigh'nn dhachaidh
l' a leòin à Inbhir-Chèitein.

You were in the Ross of Mull
like an unyielding MacLean,
like Lame Hector come home
with his wounds from Inverkeithing.
(pp. 270–271)

Mull was the traditional clan-land of the MacLeans and
An Ros Muileach/the Ross of Mull is the south-west promon-
tory of Mull. Few MacLeans returned to Mull after the Battle
of Inverkeithing on 20th July 1651, where a detachment of
Leslie's Royalist army was defeated by Lambert and nearly
700 MacLeans were killed. Sorley MacLean is suggesting
that the nobility and heroism of their ancestors has filtered
down through the generations to Calum, who was himself
of a steadfast nature, to undertake the work that he did. He
is also showing his belief that collecting folklore is a worthy
pursuit, in keeping with a MacLean.

However, the naming of many geographical locations also
serves another function in this poem and one which adds
another facet to the personal praise of his brother. In stanza
12 Irish place-names such as 'Ceathramh Ruadh is Spideal/
Cararoe and Spideal', places in Co. Galway, show the Irish
connection which Calum MacLean nurtured when he developed particular skill in the Connaught Irish dialect and in
the next stanza MacLean writes:

Dhearbh thu ann an Sealtainn
agus anns an t-Suain
agus ann an Lochlann
nach eil seirbhe anns a' chuan;
nach eil sa' ghamhlas ach facal
a thachdas fìrinn bhuan.
On bu mhùirnean thu do 'n Ghàidheal
bu mhùirnean thu do 'n Ghall.

You proved in Shetland
and in Sweden
and in Norway
that there is no bitterness in the sea;
that the 'malice' is only a word
that chokes lasting truth.
Since you were a favourite with the Gael
you were a favourite with the Gall.
(pp. 268–269)

From the summer of 1951 to the autumn of 1952, Calum
MacLean was based at Uppsala University in Sweden where
he received professional training in folklore methodology,
archival techniques and cataloguing. His index system for
the School of Scottish Studies was based on the one devised
by Professor Dag Strömbäck from Uppsala. From one
perspective, MacLean is alluding to his brother's work and in
particular, the distance he journeyed, using place-names to
achieve a sense of movement to mirror Calum's own travels.
Underlying this is the sense that this poem is also a cele-
bration of not only Scottish Gaelic connections with Gaelic
Ireland, but also the links the Gaels have to Scandinavia.
Calum MacLean's folklore collecting becomes a symbol of the
bonds between nations and this friendship and commonality
that exists in the poet's mind. The repetition of the smaller
island-scale unity between Skye and South Uist, because of
the shared connection with Calum MacLean, is reflected on a
country scale with the mention of Sweden and Norway.

Conclusion and Further Reading
'Cumha Chaluim Iain MhicGill-Eain/ Elegy for Calum I.
MacLean' is a positive reminder of the power of individual
people, the value of transference of knowledge and storytell-
ing and the importance of sense of place. Rather than emphasising borders and distinctive features, the poet highlights
the shared language of communication and the kindness and
love that can be generated from this exchange. This poem
may be an elegy for his brother, but it is also an elegy for
the tradition-bearers of his society – 'Dh'fhalbh mòran dhe

do chàirdean,/mòran de dh'uaislean nan Gàidheal / Many of your friends are gone,/many of the great ones of the Gaels' (pp. 268–269) – as well as a rallying cry for the preservation of the folklore and wisdom of his own and others' culture.

Comparisons can be drawn between 'Cumha Chaluim Iain MhicGill-Eain/ Elegy for Calum I. MacLean' and MacLean's poem, 'Do Uilleam MacMhathain/ To William Matheson'(pp. 246–247). William Matheson (1910–1995) was Senior Lecturer in Celtic at the University of Edinburgh and was the Chief of the Gaelic Society of Inverness in 1968, the same time that Sorley MacLean was their Bard. Although not an elegy, this poem could be described as a praise poem in which MacLean uses Gaelic literary and historical references in the context of his friend, who was extremely knowledgeable on Gaelic song, history and genealogy. He invests the poem with a beautiful timelessness in which the figures of Gaelic song are as alive for the poet as William Matheson himself. This is an obvious and deliberate reflection of Matheson's teaching methods and ability to convey information to his audience. MacLean describes him as 'a'chairt-iùil/ the compass' in relation to his skill at navigating people around the Gaelic literary world and thus MacLean once again shows a respect for the transmission of knowledge and scholarly research in the same way that he praises the folk collecting his brother carried out. It is likely that MacLean viewed the work these men did as being inextricably bound up with his own role as a poet. These professions all rely, and place a great deal of significance, on the Gaelic tradition, which is a rich store-house of myth, motif and symbol.

CONCLUSION

The far-reaching influence of Sorley MacLean's poetry on Gaelic as well as non-Gaelic poets is perhaps only now beginning to be fully appreciated. It is clear that his full potential and poetic range is best understood when he is assessed within both a Gaelic and European context. This is because MacLean was a poet with a foot placed firmly in each world – from MacLean's viewpoint there were never two 'worlds' anyway. Even this brief study of the span of his poetry has shown that he did not view Gaelic as an inward looking tradition but instead saw it as a culture which could interact and function in a full and rich way within the sphere of modern politics and philosophy. This belief alone has done immeasurable good for the cause of the Gaelic language and has ensured that its 20th century literary history can be viewed as a tradition which is alive with possibility. It has been almost seven decades since *Dàin do Eimhir agus Dàin Eile* was first published and began to seep into the public's consciousness and yet, in many ways, this poetry is as fresh as it was in 1943, simply because underlying all of MacLean's poetry is a belief system which is based on the hopes for the integrity of mankind, the striving for the fulfilment of potential and the belief in the redemptive powers of love and self-sacrifice. These concepts are as important and vital in this current time as they were in MacLean's own lifetime. MacLean has written in 'Hallaig' that 'chunnacas na mairbh beò/ the dead have been seen alive'. MacLean did not just resurrect Gaelic poetry or reanimate what is sometimes wrongly judged to be a dead literature, ensuring that it survived into a new century – he also breathed new life into his tradition. If we imagine his poems as trees, it is clear that he has repopulated the wood and perhaps introduced some new varieties of flora which can exist alongside the birch, the hazel and the rowan in 'coille mo ghràidh/ the wood I love.'

SELECT BIBLIOGRAPHY

Burnett, Ray, Sorley MacLean's 'Hallaig'. *Lines Review*, 92 (1985) 13–22.

Caird, J.B., 'Sorley MacLean: A Personal View' in *Sorley MacLean: Critical Essays*. ed. by Raymond J. Ross and Joy Hendry. Edinburgh: Scottish Academic Press, 1986. 39–43.

Eliot, T.S., 'Tradition and the Individual Talent' in *The Sacred Wood: Essays on Poetry and Criticism*. London: Methuen, 1920. 42–53.

Glen, Duncan, *Hugh MacDiarmid and the Scottish Renaissance*. Edinburgh: W. & R. Chambers Ltd, 1964.

Hendry, Joy, 'Sorley MacLean: The Man and his Work' in *Sorley MacLean: Critical Essays*. ed. by Raymond J. Ross and Joy Hendry. Edinburgh: Scottish Academic Press, 1986. 9–38.

MacInnes, John, 'A Radically Traditional Voice: Sorley MacLean and the Evangelical Background' in *Dùthchas nan Gàidheal: Selected Essays of John MacInnes* ed. by Michael Newton. Edinburgh: Birlinn, 2006. 381–391.

MacInnes, John, 'Sorley MacLean's Hallaig: a note' in *Dùthchas nan Gàidheal: Selected Essays of John MacInnes* ed. by Michael Newton. Edinburgh: Birlinn, 2006. 418–421.

MacInnes, John, 'Religion in Gaelic Society' in *Dùthchas nan Gàidheal: Selected Essays of John MacInnes* ed. by Michael Newton. Edinburgh: Birlinn, 2006. 425–442.

MacLean, Sorley and Robert Garioch, *17 Poems for 6d*. Edinburgh: Chalmers Press, 1940.

MacLean, Sorley, *Dàin do Eimhir agus Dàin Eile*. Glasgow: William Maclellan, 1943.

MacLean, Sorley, *Reothairt is Contraigh: Taghadh de Dhàin 1932–72/ Spring tide and Neap tide: Selected Poems 1932–72*. Edinburgh: Canongate, 1977.

MacLean, Sorley, 'My Relationship with the Muse' in *Ris a' Bhruthaich: The Criticism and Prose Writings of Sorley MacLean* ed. by William Gillies. Stornoway: Acair, 1985. 6–14.

MacLean, Sorley, *O Choille gu Bearradh/ From Wood to Ridge: Collected Poems.* Edinburgh: Carcanet/Birlinn, 1999.

MacLellan, C.A., Review of *Spring Tide and Neap Tide/ Reothairt is Contraigh: Selected Poems 1932–72. Lines Review,* 61 (1971) 44–46.

Martin, Augustine (ed.), *W.B. Yeats: Collected Poems.* London: Vintage, 1992.

Sealy, Douglas, 'Out from Skye to the World: Literature, History and the Poet' in *Sorley MacLean: Critical Essays* ed. by Raymond J. Ross and Joy Hendry. Edinburgh: Scottish Academic Press, 1986. 53–79.

Whyte, Christopher (ed.), *Somhairle MacGill-Eain/Sorley MacLean: Dàin do Eimhir.* Glasgow: The Association for Scottish Literary Studies, 2002.

CD

15 Poems of Sorley MacLean Readings by Sorley MacLean with commentary by Iain Crichton Smith. Glasgow: Association for Scottish Literary Studies, 2006

Lightning Source UK Ltd.
Milton Keynes UK

172588UK00001B/25/P